Forged by War
A Daughter Shaped by a WWII POW Story

Candie Blankman

Lyrics *Another Soldier's Going Home*, all rights reserved, used by permission of BMM Music and Maplesong Music.

The Hell Ship, painting by permission of Ben Steele

Photographs by Candie Blankman

Archive photos, public domain

Brainerd Daily Dispatch photos reproduced with the permission of The Brainerd Dispatch, www.brainerddispatch.com

Lake County Echo photo, used by permission of www.pineandlakes.com

Death March route map, used by permission of www.mapsbymikereagan.com

Letter from Danny DeArmis, used by permission of Danny DeArmis

Email from Karalyn Renaud, used by permission of Karalyn Renaud

ISBN 13: 978-1467991490
ISBN 10: 146799149X

Cover design by Anne Blankman
Drawings and oil paintings by Candie Blankman
Book Production: Karen Porter, *k*ae Creative Solutions,
www.kaecreativesolutions.com

Dedicated to my children, Jeff, Anne, and Jamie; and to my brother and sisters, Ken, Carol, Kathy, and Kari; and to their children. May they all pass the story on.

CONTENTS

Acknowledgments

Many thanks to the Lily Foundation for their Pastor Sabbatical program funding that made possible my travels to the places my father was held prisoner. Emma Wyatt, Marcia Agema, and Dr. Wayne Wilcox provided additional financial support. First Presbyterian Church of Downey, California, contributed significantly through their support of my taking sabbatical leave.

Special thanks for the encouragement and help of early readers Joan Tyvoll, Jerry and Marcia Agema, and my brother Ken who helped to shape the unique form of the book.

Words cannot adequately express my gratefulness for my children's send-off as demonstrated in their send-off notes. Also, to my daughter Anne for the cover design and other graphic assistance.

The book never would have actually made it to the publisher without the able assistance of Karen Porter in editing and formatting. Her enthusiastic and gracious encouragement took the project from *almost* complete to complete.

And last but not least to my husband of thirty-six years, who supported me all along the way beginning in the early days of recording and researching my father's story, in the adventure of retracing his steps, and in these last two years when all my spare time was given to the completion of this book.

About the Cover

My daughter Anne designed the cover of this book. It was also a labor of love. The background of the cover is taken from a telegram my paternal grandmother sent to my father when he was still a prisoner of war (see picture page 103). It was returned to sender. When I began writing my father's story my mother gave me two of these returned telegrams. Anne is a graphic artist and with her talents and the wonders of modern technology, she was able to use my grandmother's handwriting from this telegram as the font for the title and my name on the cover of the book. Amazing! The picture is of my father and me when he was 35 and I was about a year old.

My children sent me off on my sabbatical journey to the Philippine Islands and Japan with these words written in the front of a journal they gave me on February 13, 2010:

From Jeff
God's Path

> His path led him through barracks
>> A grin and quick hand
>> Served him well there
> His path led him through Bataan;
>> No shackles nor unslake
>> Were too much to bear.
> His path led him through bars and beriberi;
>> His grin may have muted,
>> But working hands stayed his end.
> His path led him through hospital bed and life with Miss Brown;
>> No bitterness nor guile there
>> But a big grin again.
> All of these places
> God's path led him through;
> Scathed but unshaken
> But unwritten, too.
> Now his path is your path
> So follow it true;
> To tell what's unspoken;
> May God bless it to you.

Love,
Jeff

From Anne
Grandpa went through more pain than I'll ever know and was the most joyous man I have ever and probably will ever meet. One of the reasons you are such an amazing woman is because you are your father's daughter. I love you both so much and am blessed to be a part of him and a part of you.
Love,
Anne

From Jamie

I am excited for you to start this new part of your journey of looking into Grandpa's journey. God has been intricately woven into the story of both your lives. I pray that God will continue to receive all the glory and change the lives of many others as you discover and share more of Grandpa's and your story; and that you will be blessed and fulfilled in countless ways. I am so grateful for both of your examples!

Love,

Jamie

Introduction

I did not know much about my father's war experience until I read about it in a newspaper when I was a junior in high school. He never talked about the war. But our family cut its teeth on his pain. The following is my story of our family forged by war and particularly how significantly I was shaped by my father's experience. I did not fully understand or value the heritage until I was in my late twenties and early thirties. I studied history in college and became a social studies teacher. So I invited my father to talk to my sophomore American history classes about his experience as a POW. As he regaled the students with his stories, I stood in the back of the room and cried. I had never heard so much of the story myself. He never stopped talking about it after that day.

After serving a year and a half as a regimental draftsman at the Quartermaster Headquarters Company, First Command Post, in Manila, he spent three and a half years in prison camps in the Philippine Islands and Japan. He survived the Bataan Death March (See paintings page 24 and 41), two POW camps, a hell ship, and hard labor in a Japanese copper mine. When he enlisted, he was nineteen years old, stood five feet seven inches tall and weighed one hundred sixty-five pounds (See photo page 89). He was much "older" and weighed a mere 90 pounds when he was liberated (See painting page 173). He had seen more life and death in those three and a half years than he would see in the next sixty. He was profoundly affected by these years. So was I. Our whole family was.

Kenneth E. Davis met Hazel Irene Brown when he returned to his hometown near Brainerd, Minnesota, in the fall of 1945. Three months later, on February 20, 1946, they were married (See photos page 99).

A doctor told my father he would never have children. The malnutrition combined with malaria, beriberi, and acute dysentery had ravaged his young body. On November 15, 1946, eight months and twenty-five days after my father and mother were married, my brother, Kenneth Jr. was born. Five more of us followed in the next twenty-two years. Carol was born July 26, 1948. Three years after Carol, my mother miscarried (the baby would have been named Kevin). April 13, 1954, Kathy was born. I came along sixteen months later, on August 22, 1955. And on February 13, 1968, when my POW father was almost forty-seven, he fathered his sixth child, Kari. With five living children, twelve grandchildren, and thirteen great-grandchildren, my father obviously proved the doctor wrong.

Though my father's diseases and his experiences as a prisoner of war did not render him sterile, they deeply affected him and our family. Hardly a day went by that our family did not feel the results of his imprisonment. Every meal contained the signs. Every prayer whispered the truth. And every person he met benefited from his suffering. For my sisters and brother, each day reflected the lessons learned. Each of us have our own unique story to tell about how Dad influenced us and how we experienced him as a father. We are a family forged by war.

Tom Brokaw described the people of the World War II era as the "Greatest Generation." These veterans built homes and families on the memories of the war. More POWs came home from WWII than any other war, but the country couldn't and didn't handle these former prisoners well. The soldiers were examined and as soon as each one reached a weight near normal, they were sent home. These men and women brought home medals and were greeted by parades and fanfare, but for years they were not asked about their war experiences. There weren't enough counselors, psychiatrists, or psychologists to listen. Dad's sister, Ruthie Renquist, said when the family was preparing to see Dad after he returned to the United States and had spent a couple of months in military hospitals, they were instructed not to ask him about his war experiences. The country was ill-prepared to hear what they had suffered.

Times change. My generation is a reflective and inquisitive one. So in 1988 I began to ask Dad about his experience. I talked to him regularly about being a soldier and a prisoner of war. I listened. And I recorded his answers. For almost ten years, each time I visited I asked questions and took notes. Then I would send him the results and let him correct any errors or misunderstandings. As I poured back over those notes to write the story, I grieved again his loss. I have so many more questions. I didn't have time to ask them all. And now, twenty years later, having traveled to the places where he suffered as a POW, my heart cries out to talk to him.

This family album is chiefly the result of the conversations I had with Dad, but it is enhanced by the journey I took in February and March 2010 to visit the places where he fought and was held as prisoner. In 1999 he was diagnosed with Alzheimer's disease. By 2004 he no longer spoke of or remembered his war experiences. He didn't remember he was a World War II hero. In his final years he no longer recognized me. The man who survived the Death March, death camps, a hell ship, and forced labor did not survive Alzheimer's. My father, Kenneth Earl Davis, passed away on April 18, 2006, after spending his last two and a half years in a veteran's hospital in Tomah, Wisconsin (See photo page 100).

Ten years of conversation about an extraordinary life is now mine to pass on to my children and grandchildren. I hope they will pay attention at an earlier age than I did. I hope those who read the account will gain a deeper appreciation for the life experiences that forged their own families. Mine was forged by war.

1 Take All You Want

"Take all you want, but eat all you take." Every meal in our home began this way. It didn't matter whether it was just two or three of us at the table, or if we had twenty-five guests for a picnic. Every meal began with my father praying and giving thanks for the food, which always ended with "Bless this food to our bodies and us to thy service. Amen." Then, without a pause Dad would proclaim the rules of engagement — "Take all you want, but eat all you take."

My father's attitude toward the gift of food was one of the last things to go when he was diagnosed with Alzheimer's in 1999. Once when I visited him, he asked how I was related to him.

I said, "I am your daughter."

When I left the room he asked my mother again, "How am I related to her?"

My mother said, "She is our daughter."

My father responded, "How can she be our daughter when we don't have any children?"

We could only laugh. The alternative was to cry. The disease had stolen his memories. However, when we sat down to eat that same evening, my father began as he always had, thanking God for the food and asking God to bless it. After he said "Amen," he looked at me and said, "Take all you want, but eat all you take."

As a child I did not understand where the obsession with eating everything on my plate came from. I just knew food was not to be thrown away. If our "eyes were bigger than our bellies," as my father would say when one of us put more food on our plate than we could eat, we remained at the table until our bellies made room. Once in a while Dad would help. He removed the punishment and shame from us by taking what was left on our plate and eating it himself. I was always grateful when he ate my food, but I had no idea how much more grateful my father was. After living for almost four years on next to nothing, second and third helpings of food were like gold to him.

I watched and learned. When I had children of my own, I took up the charge. For me it manifested itself in several ways. Though I didn't start the meal with my father's mantra, I often would not serve myself any food at all. I waited until my children were done and ate what they didn't. And I am notorious for putting leftovers, no matter how small, in the refrigerator only to be thrown away a few days later. But at least I tried! The value of food I learned from my father also affected what I taught my children in the language they used. When Americans are hungry they often say, "I'm starving!" Not my children and not in my house. I repeatedly told them, "You don't know what it's like to be starving. You may be hungry, but you are *not* starving! There are people for whom starvation is a daily experience, and your grandpa Davis was one of them."

My father enlisted in the U.S. Army on September 9, 1940. He was assigned to the 31st Infantry, and in October of the same year was sent to the Philippine Islands. He was a regimental draftsman and trained as a fixed-radio operator. He served at the Quartermaster Headquarters Company First Command Post at Cuartel de Espana just north of Manila.[1]

---

[1]In the transcripts from conversations with my father, he always referred to his station in the Philippines as being in Roosevelt Park. Roger Mansell, founder and director of the Center for Research Allied POW's Under the Japanese, said there was no such station and that Roosevelt Park was just a "bump in the road." According to the records Mansell found, Dad was assigned to the command post at Cuartel de Espana. I inquired about this post to another POW named Smith L. Green. In an email dated November 11, 2010, he said, "I visited the Cuartel de Espana which was a pile of rubble. Even the walls of the Intramuros (old walled city) were blown down by bombs and artillery shells. We had left our footlockers and wall lockers full of our possessions. We fully expected to return after we had disposed of the Japs! I also visited some of our old haunts. Same. Manila was really torn up."

Dad's honorable discharge papers describe his MOS (military operational specialty).

> As a member of Headquarters Company, 31st Infantry, prepared clear, complete and accurate working plans and detailed drawings from sketches and suggested notes from command. Also made proposed drawings and maps of possible enemy locations and friendly locations to be used in planning offensive and defensive engagements. Used drafting equipment. Had knowledge of mechanical, structural and topographical drawing. Also knew the materials and mathematics to complete drawing. Was familiar with blueprints and photo static copies. Served in the Philippines in the capacity for 18 months up to the time of capture on Bataan, April 9th, 1942[2] (See documents pages 105, 106, and 107).

Less than fourteen months later the Japanese bombed the U.S. naval base at Pearl Harbor, or Pu'uloa, a lagoon harbor west of Honolulu, on the island of Oahu, Hawaii. The 31st Infantry stationed on the island of Luzon, Philippine Islands, was informed the Japanese would begin exerting pressure on the islands within forty-two hours. On December 8, after destroying more than half of all the U.S. air support parked on Clark Airfield, located forty miles northwest of Manila, the Japanese landed on the northern coast of Luzon. On December 12 they landed in southern Luzon at Legazpi. Then the main invasion began on December 22 with a three-point landing at Lingayen Gulf.[3] My father, along with the 31st Infantry, was ordered to Bataan to set up a line of defense at Orani.

---

[2]Separation Qualification Record, Army of the United States Honorable Discharge papers, p. 2.

[3]"Philippines Campaign 1941-42," *Wikipedia*, July 5, 2010, http://en.wikipedia.org/wiki/Philippines_Campaign_(1941%E2%80%931942).

Two more times they were ordered to retreat to a new line of defense, each time cutting themselves off more from access to supplies. And so the rationing began.[4]

Early on they were at half rations and under constant siege, with little time for sleep. By the time the U.S. and Filipino infantry had retreated to Mariveles, at the southernmost point of the Bataan Peninsula, there was little left to ration. After almost four months of fierce fighting, little sleep, and little food, the troops were malnourished and most were already seriously ill.[5] Many had contracted malaria. Most had dysentery.

Disease and starvation was hardship enough for any soldier to endure, but it did not end there. On April 12, 1942, three days after the troops were ordered by General Douglas MacArthur and Major General Edward King to surrender, the Japanese began marching these malnourished and sick men in the scorching heat of the spring sun—without water or food. The march later came to be known as the Bataan Death March. An estimated ten thousand to seventeen thousand men died on the march.

Over the next fourteen days my father, along with an estimated seventy thousand other men, marched up to sixty miles, depending on where they joined the march.

> Filipino and American prisoners were coming down from the mountain trails onto the main road along Manila Bay. The groups swelled so that any order became impossible. Already the day's march from Cabcaben had begun to take its toll.

---

[4]"The half ration was inaugurated 6 January. In terms of energy units the ration averaged 2000 calories during January, 1,500 calories during February, and 1,000 calories during March. The nature of the terrain in which the defense of Bataan was conducted required, conservatively estimated, an energy output of from 3500-4000 calories per man per day. By 1 March, serious muscle wasting was evident. The ration was deficient in vitamins A, B, and C and beriberi became universal. The low rations, in combination with malnutrition, was the cause of thousands of hospitalizations" (Paul Reiter, "G-4 and Surgeon of Luzon Force Report," *Battling Bastards of Bataan*, January 1998, http://home.pacbell.net/fbaldie/BattlingBastardsof Bataan.html).

[5]"By April 1, 1942, the combat efficiency was rapidly approaching the zero point" (Ibid.).

Prisoners slumped to the ground. Some, in a daze, rested and got to their feet where they fell. Some prisoners began to drink from the occasional carabao wallows—green and skummed over and sometimes fouled by the bloated body of a dead Japanese or Filipino or American soldier. However, the terrible thirst combined with malaria or dengue fever made prisoners forget the consequences of drinking such water—usually dysentery.[6]

Each group marched for five to nine days with only occasional stops, and most without any food or water. Artesian wells lined the road, but prisoners were not allowed to stop for a drink—which amounted to torture. Those who did stop were shot in the attempt and often bayoneted or worse, decapitated. Dead and swollen bodies lined the march route. Intensifying the torture, the marchers often passed contingents of Japanese soldiers who purposefully stopped along the route for meal breaks to taunt the starving prisoners marching past (See photo page 91).

Though the deprivation was severe, it got worse. For the next three and a half years my father, along with thousands of other men, would often only see two or three tablespoons of uncooked rice each day and perhaps a cup of water to be shared with countless men one teaspoon at a time. Occasionally there would be cooked rice. But it was watered down and often full of who knows what. The rice was "moving"—full of bugs and vermin.

When Dad was finally released from Schick General Hospital in Clinton, Iowa, sometime in November, 1945, he took a bus home to Brainerd, Minnesota. There his sister Ruthie met him. Later that week his sister Patty had him over for dinner. Half-way through the meal she realized, with no small amount of horror, that she had fixed him rice. She apologized profusely. What was she thinking! Dad reassured her that it was not a problem. He loved rice. It had saved his life. And besides, he told her, "The rice doesn't crawl off the plate!"[7]

---

[6]Bernard Fitzpatrick, quoted in "Bataan," *Minneapolis Tribune*, April 19, 1981, 2E.

[7]Taken from a conversation I had in the late 1990s with Patty Jewel, my dad's sister, retold again in February 2010.

When Dad first returned to the United States he was examined and treated in Seattle, Washington, at Fort Lewis and the Madigan Medical Center. His brother Wally and Wally's wife, Minnie, lived in the Seattle area. And his brother Francis and sister Ruthie came to Seattle to see Dad. They were all at Wally and Minnie's for a fried chicken and cream gravy dinner—Dad's request. While they were waiting for dinner, Minnie came into the living room and asked if there was anything she could get Dad. He thought for only a second and then asked if she had any lettuce. She said she did and asked if he would like her to cut some up on a plate for him. He said, "No. Just bring me the head," which she did. Dad thanked her and commenced to eat the entire head of lettuce.[8] Dad had not seen fresh lettuce or fresh green vegetables for almost four years. The lettuce tasted like dessert.

These men were so starved as prisoners they would eat anything. Grass and bugs were a delicacy, if they could be found. My father remembered a locust swarm coming into one of the camps. It shut down all the work details, and their Japanese captors disappeared from sight as they sheltered themselves from the swarms. Though a nightmare for them, it was manna from heaven for the prisoners! They caught, cooked, and ate all the locusts they could capture—legs and all. My father understood what it means to be starving.

Dad enlisted weighing one hundred sixty five pounds. In September, 1945 when he was liberated from Sendai No. 6 (Hanawa) in the north of Honshu, Japan, he weighed about ninety pounds. He knew starvation. I have not known starvation. Neither have my children. Few Americans have. I couldn't allow my children to use the expression "I'm starving" casually. It was not casual. It was real. Living with my father taught me that.

Besides being a grateful eater, Dad was also a fast eater. He wasted no time digging in to whatever was served. There was no pause for conversation. There was no discussion about the food. It was time to eat, and eat he did! He was always the first to clean his plate, often long before the rest of us had made a dent in the food on our plates. My father later explained to me that

---

[8]Story told to me by Ruthie Renquist, my father's sister, in May 2010.

when the prisoners did get food, they ate very quickly. Besides their obvious hunger, there was the real possibility that if they hesitated someone would grab and eat it. He also explained they ate their rations quickly, especially at night; otherwise the large lice they hosted would eat it first! Dad's speed-eating too was a result of starvation.

It took me into my twenties and thirties, having studied to be a teacher of American history, to understand my father's obsession with eating everything on his plate. I wanted my children to know sooner than I did how blessed they were not to know starvation. I think they learned it very early in life. I wasn't as faithful as my father, so it didn't occur at every meal, but often when we all gather for a meal now, one of our now adult children will say, "Take all you want, but eat all you take."

My father's gratefulness was not limited to mealtime and the food on our plates. His experience with scarcity as a POW forged a man who took nothing for granted. Everything was a gift from God to be thankful for and then to savor. Everything in life was to be appreciated and shared with those who had less. Every piece of wood from a fallen tree, every drop of water from the hose, every breath taken was to be used to its fullest and to share with others. Even though our family was relatively poor by American standards, my father's POW experience forged a way of living and created a sense that we had most things in abundance. As a result of his attitude and example, I didn't know that we were poor until much later in life. But now I realize that we *weren't* poor. We were rich in things that cannot be taken away. Being raised by a father who had everything taken away, we knew a different kind of richness. So to this day, not only with food but with many other of life's resources, I try to remember to take all I want, but eat all I take.

DEATH MARCH INSTIGATOR
Oil Painting, 2009

2   Combat up Close and Personal

On December 7, 1941, the American naval fleet at Pearl Harbor had been bombed and decimated. President Franklin D. Roosevelt proclaimed the day as "a date which will live in infamy." The attack jolted the United States out of its isolationist cocoon and catapulted the country into a full-scale world war. A day later, on December 8, the Japanese bombed Clark Airfield on Luzon, northwest of Manila. Consequently, most of the air support for the Philippine Islands was destroyed. The American generals knew the Japanese had plans to seize control of the Pacific. They hoped the battle for the Philippines would delay the Japanese long enough to allow the American military to rebuild and recruit for all-out war. So began the battle for Bataan. MacArthur ordered the troops to retreat to Bataan and prepare to confront the Japanese forces which were already beginning their assault on the Philippines.

One of Dad's commanders, Colonel Charles Steel, ordered the troops at Roosevelt Park[9] to move south toward Bataan, near Orani (See photo page 91), to higher ground for better observation. They arrived there in the morning and began setting up tents and a command post from which they could easily watch a nearby highway. Just after military cooks came to the command post with the evening meal and the soldiers had begun to eat, an artillery officer came into the camp and asked for the colonel, saying, "Japs are coming four abreast, pulling field artillery." Steel replied, "For God's sake, I'm not running your business, but get back to the artillery post and fire on them!"

---

[9]Another reference my father made to Roosevelt Park. The particular reference could have been a temporary encampment at the beginning of the retreat to the Bataan Peninsula.

Five or ten minutes later they heard artillery and what sounded like a direct hit. Then the artillery stopped. Later it was learned the direct hit was on the advancing Japanese, but because the artillery commander let up, the Japanese soldiers kept coming. Then the U.S. soldiers began to hear overhead shrapnel and what sounded like small-arms fire from the south. Everyone got into their command post dugouts. This battle was the first time my father experienced gunfire.

I know this idea may seem silly, but I remember being very surprised to hear my father talk about being under fire and carrying a rifle and shooting. Somehow in my idyllic view of the world and my father, I had envisioned he was a military radio operator one day and a POW the next. I had never imagined or asked him about his experience in combat because I didn't know about the four months of battle that ensued before Bataan fell. When my father described his experience in live combat, the interview came to a sudden stop. I heard for the first time that my father had been shot at and fired back. My dad, who was as sweet and as kind and peaceful as any man could be, had been in live combat!

No longer in the interview mode, but now with intense curiosity and wonder, the question just came out. I was no longer the adult daughter getting the record straight for posterity. Now I was a little girl asking my hero, my father, a question. I asked him if he had ever killed anyone. He was clearly uncomfortable with the question. But he responded quickly, "I never stopped to check." The early days in the defense of Bataan was only the beginning of almost four years of my dad's battle to survive. There was no looking back.

During the initial assault on Bataan my father decided to move to a covered dugout, but he found it disconcerting to not be able to look around, so he returned to an open dugout. The U.S. soldiers assumed they were surrounded and were told to "grab their rifles." They crawled up an incline to a crest. Upon reaching the crest they discovered the small arms fire was their own ammunition truck, which had been hit by shrapnel.

Dad remembered his unit being instructed to move south again. They were sent to Balanga, called Abucay Hacienda, which means "avocado orchard," to set up a defense line on higher ground. All the troops pulled out crawling and keeping cover because enemy gunfire was coming from both sides. Maneuvering undercover they came upon the avocado orchard. Taking fire continually, they stayed in the shelter of the orchard until the next day.

> The ninety thousand U.S. and Filipino troops were defending Bataan. The main defense line (roughly from Mauban to Abucay) was organized into two corps. The western corps was under the leadership of Major General Jonathan Wainwright; the eastern corps was under the leadership of Major General George Parker. Wainwright's troops consisted of three Philippine Divisions (1st, 31st, 91st) and the 26th Cavalry. Parker's troops comprised four Philippine Divisions (11th, 21st, 41st, 51st) and a Philippine Scout Division (57th).

> The U.S. troops outnumbered the Japanese on Bataan. But they were at a decided disadvantage: they were on half rations, they were short on medical supplies, and many had contracted beriberi, dysentery, and malaria. Besides that, they [the eastern and western corps] were divided by the four-thousand foot Mt. Natib and communication lines were poor.

> According to Major Gordon, "Food supplies stored on Corregidor often never found their way to the front lines in Bataan, being stolen by hungry rear area troops while the food was en route in trucks. Hijacking became a common practice along the way. Here may be found the first difference between Bataan and Corregidor. Corregidor troops did not go hungry until their capture by the Japanese. Consequently, the men of Corregidor entered captivity in relatively good health and with very few cases of malaria on record."

> On January 9, 1942, the Japanese attacked the U.S. defense line on Bataan. The U.S. troops held for six days. Then the Japanese

broke through the 51st Division on the east. Counter attacks didn't help. By January 21, Wainwright's divisions were in trouble. MacArthur ordered a general withdrawal to a second defense line eight miles south on January 24. The line ran across the peninsula from Bagac to Orion. [10]

Dad remembered the U.S. troops were given orders a third time to move south again to form another line of defense (this must be the Bagac to Orion line). The soldiers found higher ground and dug individual foxholes, which were well spread out. Then they called for help from a tank battalion via radio. They knew Japanese air forces could intercept these transmissions, so from then on messengers were sent regarding withdrawal movement. The troops had encountered a bamboo grove "full of Japanese." The tanks were needed to shell the grove in swale with infantry behind to clear it out. When the Japanese soldiers encountered the tanks, they hollered, "*Bonsai!*" crawled up on the tanks and tried to open the covers with their bayonets. Many were killed before they reached the tanks. The rest were shot off the tanks by the infantry.

During this sequence of events a motorcycle came in with a message. A commander instructed Dad and fellow soldier Jackson to flush out some snipers who had fired on the motorcycle as it was coming in. Dad and Jackson were unable to find the snipers and returned to the camp. The commander then told them to find the Filipino 31st Infantry and not return until they did so. The order the messenger had brought in sent Jackson and my father out and within five miles they encountered the 31st Infantry.

Eventually the Japanese withdrew from the grove, but a nearby sugarcane farm posed a similar problem. About twelve scouts were sent to check it out. Apparently the Japanese let them go through the grove unharmed in order to lower their guard; then they fired on the scouts as they returned through the grove.

Eight of the scouts survived to report the Japanese were in the sugarcane farm.

---

[10]Battling Bastards of Bataan website.

In order to literally smoke them out, the Americans set fire to the sugarcane. The Japanese soldiers who survived the fire retreated out of the back of the grove.

> By this time, the Japanese had suffered almost 25 percent casualties, but they launched a frontal attack with three amphibious landings on the southwest corner of the peninsula behind the American lines. The U.S. forces held. Under the present conditions, the Japanese forces were no longer capable of mounting an extended attack. Therefore, from February 8 to April 3, 1942, the Japanese laid siege to Bataan, waiting for reinforcements and supplies.[11]

> On 22 February, President Roosevelt ordered MacArthur to Australia. MacArthur resisted the order but finally obeyed and left Corregidor on March 11 (by PT boat). General Wainwright took command at Corregidor and assumed control of the U.S. forces. Major General Edward King took command of the troops on Bataan. At this point the U.S. troops' rations were reduced to one thousand calories per day. By late March, General King determined the U.S. forces could only fight at 30 percent of their efficiency. At the same time, Japanese forces had been resupplied and reinforced. The Japanese attacked early on April 3, and the U.S. defense line collapsed almost immediately; they had to withdraw and regroup. King surrendered on April 9.[12]

My father recalled the troops stayed on the defense line near Orion until the pressure from the Japanese was too great. Once again they had to withdraw to higher ground to set up a new line of defense.

---

[11]David Smurthwaite, *Pacific War Atlas, 1941-1945* (New York: Facts on File, 1995), pp. 43-44

[12]Ibid., p. 44.

Withdrawal was always at night. During one withdrawal the trucks did not use their headlights, and one tail-light from each truck was unhooked. The tail-lights were unhooked to prevent the enemy from easily spotting them. The drivers of the trucks simply followed the glowing tail light of the truck in front of them.

One night during withdrawal and while rounding a curve, a Jeep carrying a captain, Jackson, Dad, a Filipino interpreter, and the driver went off the road, falling twelve to fourteen feet down a bank into a bamboo grove. The truck rolled. Hearing no noise from his mates, Dad crawled up the embankment. He stopped the next truck in the convoy to get help for the other men in the Jeep and to warn the convoy about the dangerous spot in the road. As Dad was talking to those in the truck he fell to the ground unconscious. Medics came, tended to Dad, found the others, who were not injured, and transported my father, who could no longer move his body, to a field hospital. He remained under care at the field hospital until the next day, when he was released. The apparent cause of his paralysis was shock. True to form my father reflected on a positive side to the accident—the command car that overturned was full of hand grenades in the back and it was discovered they were all duds and would not have functioned if needed.

While at the hospital Dad saw for the first time the real ravages of war. Having regained consciousness by the time he got to the hospital, he looked around. There was a captain from the 31st Infantry with his leg blown off and the bone sticking out. There was also a Filipino with his chin blown off, and the wound was crawling with maggots. Upon inquiring, Dad learned that these medical maggots were used to rid the wound of infection, thus preventing serious gangrene. An American medic explained to him that after the maggots had eaten away all of the dead and injured flesh, they were removed and the wound was packed with sulfathiazole.[13]

---

[13]"Sulfathiazole," www.wikipedia.org. Sulfathiazole is a short-acting sulfa drug. It used to be a common oral and topical antimicrobial until less toxic alternatives were discovered. It is still occasionally used, sometimes in combination with sulfabenzamide and sulfacetamide, and in aquariums. The general category of sulfa drugs used was called sulfa celinamides.

These images remained in my father's mind and were only the beginning of many horrors he was to see. Dad returned to his company the next morning, but he was not the same. The not quite twenty-one-year-old trained as a fixed radio operator and regimental draftsman had now experienced almost four months of frontline battle and had seen up close the human cost of such warfare. My father never said so directly, but I could tell by the way he talked about his experience; this episode was a shocking reality check. It was part of the foundation for his stubborn determination to survive the hell he had entered.

The next day the troops were organized to move again. The commander of Dad's regimental division told him and Jackson he figured this would be their "last stand." The troops were now very near the southern tip of the Bataan Peninsula so these orders must have been during the Japanese final attack in early April. The commander instructed Dad and Jackson that all equipment should go to the rear of the division, and they were to tell Trail A the Japanese were on the way. When they came to Trail A, mortar shelling began. These mortars are called "knee mortars" because of their propensity to do damage to soldiers' knees. Mortars were falling all around them. They had to maneuver up and down hills and in and out of cover all of the way back to the command post.

The American troops crossed a river and stopped to look at their maps. The commander asked Dad to go to the river to get water for the canteen. Everyone was instructed to take a little iodine with the water because the water was contaminated by the many dead bodies in the river. However, they had to be careful with the iodine, too, because too much of it caused the passing of blood. When they returned with the water, the command car was gone. Jackson and Dad waited, sitting on a curve in the road until another car came along. It picked them up and proceeded to a mango grove. They got out of the car and waited for their officer to return. They waited until dark, but the officer had not returned. Jackson and Dad decided to make contact with the other forces. They walked along the road until they came to another officer, named Bell, also from the 31st Infantry. There, soldiers were gathering to make another line of defense.

My father was not a violent man. He was strong and formidable, but he was gentle. He was a hunter when we lived in northern Minnesota, but he was not a "weapon-packing" kind of guy. It is just so hard for me to imagine him in this kind of combat. But hearing his story and knowing he was indeed a frontline soldier in a theater of war that took thousands of lives once again revealed a major lesson he taught me. You can't tell a person's character by an isolated incident or particular period in their life. It is the overall direction of a person's life and what he or she does with the direction that often determines character.

The time of combat in my dad's life, I believe, helped to make him the fighter he was. But he did not fight any more wars. He fought for his family and his neighbors and at times even for his enemies to have a better life and a deeper understanding of God's love for all humankind. His stubborn determination, visible in his strong body and his set jaw, which were used to help him survive the war and imprisonment, later in life were used for the good of all those who came to know him. He was a warrior. He was forged by war. But he was a warrior for good.

The song "Another Soldier's Comin' Home" by Janet Paschal was played at his memorial service during the video eulogy. The lyrics say it all.

> His back is bent and weary
> His voice is tired and low
> His sword is worn from battle
> And his steps have gotten slow
> But he used to walk on water
> Or it seemed that way to me
> I know he moved some mountains
> And never left his knees
>
> Strike up the band, assemble the choir
> Another soldier's comin' home
> Another warrior hears the call
> He's waited for so long
> He'll battle no more, he's won his war
> Make sure heaven's table

Has room for at least one more
Sing a welcome song
Another soldier's comin' home

He's faced the winds of sorrow
But his heart knows no retreat
He walked in narrow places
Knowing Christ knew no defeat
But now his steps turn homeward
So much closer to the prize
He's sounding kinda homesick
There's a longing in his eyes

Strike up the band, assemble the choir
Another soldier's comin' home
Another warrior hears the call
He's waited for so long
He'll battle no more, he's won his war
Make sure heaven's table
Has room for at least one more
Sing a welcome song
Another soldier's comin' home.
He'll battle no more, he's won his war
Make sure heaven's table
Has room for at least one more
Sing a welcome song, another soldier's comin' home.[14]

Though I miss the old soldier more than I can express, I am grateful to God he will battle no more wars, the choir and band of heaven have welcomed him, and the table is set with a place card just for him. Another soldier, my dad, has gone home.

---

[14]Janet Paschal, "Another Soldier's Comin' Home," 1997. BMM Music Inc., and Maplesong Music. All rights reserved. Used by permission.

3 Surrender or Run

The men who fought valiantly for four months against incredible odds called themselves the Battling Bastards of Bataan. They had successfully defended Bataan for more than four months when the Japanese planned on taking it in three weeks. They fought hard and long in spite of their deteriorating health due to disease and malnutrition. They held the Japanese off by establishing three different defense lines. Now their backs were against the South China Sea and there was nothing else they could do. A Captain Bell gathered the troops on the southern end of Bataan, gave out the remaining rice and said, "The jig is up." He told them they could remain and wait for possible reinforcements or were free to try to survive on their own. MacArthur gave orders from Australia to counterattack, but the commander in charge on Bataan, General King, ignored the order and surrendered on April 9, 1942. [15]

Three men—Jackson, Weber, and my father—decided in an instant to try to make it on their own. They disappeared into the jungle with the uniforms on their backs, mess kits, and rifles with bayonets. They scavenged and maneuvered for only a couple of days when they encountered a company of about two hundred American soldiers on their way to Mariveles to surrender. The three were advised there was less chance of being executed if they surrendered in large numbers and were invited to join the larger group. Since there had been no official orders to surrender, my dad and Jackson decided to remain at large. Weber joined the company surrendering.

---

[15]Battling Bastards of Bataan website.

Having worked closely with strategic maps, Dad knew where all the food depots were. He thought some of them might have been overlooked in the hurried retreat and they may even find some others heading north. He knew the search for food would bring them deeper into territory now occupied by the Japanese, but if they could get far enough north, there was a very remote area where Dad thought they would be safe. Other Allied soldiers tried this tack. Some were successful and worked alongside the Filipino guerilla forces fighting the Japanese occupation the entire duration of the war. Others were captured and executed or sent to one of the camps.

So into the jungle my father and Jackson went. During their time on the run they found a rock spring and decided to take rest and eat some of the rations they had been given, since they had not eaten for a couple of days. They still had a deck of cards and so found themselves lying by the spring playing cards. Suddenly, Jackson said to my dad, "Don't move or make a sound!" Then he said, "Don't look now but get your gun ready because there is a boar just to our left drinking from the spring." My father described how he carefully and quietly prepared his gun to make the kill. The boar was a meal just waiting to happen. The boar was unaware of the pending danger; my father pulled the trigger. "Click." The noise caught the boar's attention and it took off running. Jackson began pummeling my father for not having the gun loaded. My father opened the magazine and showed Jackson the shell still sitting in the chamber. The gun had misfired.

The next day when they were making their way north, they came upon a gaggle of birds scrounging in the grass. Just as they were preparing to claim these for dinner a very loud noise interrupted and the birds flew off. My father recognized the sound as the guns of Corregidor. The guns had been unsuccessful in helping to defend Bataan but now were quite successful in scaring off a much needed dinner.

Such was the short-lived life on the run for my father and Jackson. With no success in finding any of the food or ammunition depots, weak and sick from malaria and dysentery, the men realized they did not have a chance of making it far enough north to be out of imminent risk of capture and likely execution.

Reluctantly they decided to watch for a larger group of American and Filipino troops surrendering and join the surrender. It was clearly inevitable. They would be prisoners of war. That is, if they were not executed. Now they waited to join the surrender. Always the optimist and always hopeful, my father said that he and Jackson found a hollow tree, wrapped their guns in a tarp and hid them in the tree. My father thought perhaps they would be able to retrieve them at some point when they might be useful again.

Dad said, "I was with the last contingent of prisoners out. A Sergeant Jackson and I were the only two Americans—all the rest were Filipinos. We didn't know what was happening. We thought maybe they were killing all of the Americans."[16] After only two days on the run and after stashing their guns, without food or water they were forced to surrender.

Later in life, my father often mentioned those guns in that tree. He wondered, no, he believed if he could return to the Bataan Peninsula he could find those guns. That was my dad. He was an optimist and a believer. I only wish that I could have taken him back to try.

For many years I wondered what it would be like to visit the Philippine Islands and Japan to see the places my father talked about. Having worked for churches and nonprofits our whole lives and raising three children, my husband and I did not have extra financial resources to make the journey. Then after thirteen years in full-time ministry I learned about the sabbatical grants offered by the Lily Foundation and decided to apply. As I thought about what personally gratifying and professionally enriching thing I might do during a sabbatical, it dawned on me perhaps I could use the time to do what I had always dreamed of doing—visit the sites on the Philippine Islands and Japan where Dad was during the war.

I had started recording his story in 1988 and wanted to put all the information together in a form that would allow my children to know about their grandfather and perhaps pass it on to their own children. The more I thought

---

[16]Kenneth Davis, quoted in "Bataan," *Brainerd Daily Dispatch*, April 7, 1967, p. 1.

about it, the more I realized how much his POW experience and the way he lived afterward shaped me, not only as a person but as a pastor. As a result, my sabbatical proposal became a combination of personal journey and professional exploration. I decided to retrace my father's footsteps as prisoner of war and to spend the time away from the demands of full-time ministry writing and painting what I learned and experienced.

My first application was denied. I was devastated, but not defeated. I had inherited a good chunk of my father's stubborn determination. I submitted a somewhat modified application for a different sabbatical program funded by the Lily Foundation. It was approved, and in the spring of 2010 my dream of visiting the places he described became a reality. Being in those places was much more powerful than I had imagined. Writing about it and drawing and painting what I saw and experienced revealed just how very much I have been shaped as a person and a pastor by his influence in my life. Though I was not able to take him with me, I will be forever grateful for the opportunity to go at all.

In one of the very first sketches I did while on sabbatical, my father's presence with me showed up in a very unusual way. From a photograph I drew a picture of the beginning (00 kilometer) marker at Mariveles, Bataan, where the infamous Death March began. It was my first attempt at drawing part of the journey. I really got into it. The drawing is a close-up of the kilometer marker monument set in a small park in Mariveles. I concentrated on the marker and its aging façade with two zeroes and the F.A.M.E.[17] moniker and accompanying rendering of two men on the march, one fallen to the ground and the other reaching down to help him back up.

Then as I began drawing the background, with the grass and bushes and trees from the park surrounding it, I noticed something. At the very upper left-hand corner of the photograph was the distinct silhouette of a man standing with his hands on his hips. I had not seen him in the photo, nor when I began to draw. The image is nondescript, allowing it to be "any man." I could not help but feel the silhouette was my father watching me as I began the incredible journey.

---

[17] Filipino-American Memorial Endowment

In the drawing, (see page 41) the silhouette implies someone unnoticed and barely visible, but present. I experienced my father's presence throughout my travels. In my heart and mind he was always with me. The silhouette of his life continues to cast a shadow on everything I do.

I so wanted him to be with me. He would have loved to see the things I saw when I visited Bataan and northern Japan. And he would have loved the attention. In the Philippine Islands WWII veterans are treated like royalty. Everywhere we went there was evidence of the Filipino love for Americans, especially for General MacArthur and the troops that fought so sacrificially to defend Bataan. As I walked along the Bataan Death March route I could imagine Dad and me walking arm in arm. As I stood at the boxcar at the Capas National Monument and touched the Camp O'Donnell memorial stone erected there, how I wished that he had been standing with me and telling me more about his story from these places.

As I walked up the grassy road to the memorial at Cabanatuan I could imagine him recounting the two years he suffered there. At the Municipal City Jail in Manila, I am sure he would have been amazed to see the prison tower and some of the very same buildings were still standing exactly where they were more than sixty-five years earlier (See photos page 94). And I am sure he would have been troubled by the current condition of the jail, which meant the suffering he experienced in that place continues to this day. Looking out over Manila Harbor undoubtedly would have brought back memories for him of waiting in the hold of the *Noto Maru*, packed with so many sick and dying men wondering when and where the suffering would end.

Dad would have loved the train ride we took to the northern part of Japan. It was a new train but traveled the same route he had taken sixty-seven years earlier. When we toured the mine, I wonder if he would have been able to go into the tunnels and feel safe. He spent one bitterly cold winter there, and it was a very cold winter day when I visited. I wonder if the icy winds of winter would have brought back chilling memories of the pain and suffering he knew from that place.

As difficult as it must have been for him to remember and to describe what he endured, once he realized he had an audience it was hard to get him to stop. Dad loved to talk. I so wished he could have been there with me on the journey to do just that. Talk. I could have listened forever.

DEATH MARCH KM 00
Pencil Drawing, 2010

4 Life Flashing Before My Eyes

We have all heard the expression, "My life flashed before my eyes." It is a common way of expressing a time when a person thought he or she was going to die and felt the need to do a life inventory. In that moment when a person thinks life is about to end, it is a common experience to see the major events—for good or ill—somehow displayed in his or her mind. My father had his life-flashing-before-his-eyes experience when he was lying face down in a dry rice paddy before the infamous Bataan Death March began.

After a three-day failed attempt to escape into the jungle, my father and fellow soldier Jackson were lying on their backs in the jungle considering their options when they heard a small plane flying overhead. The Japanese used these aircraft for observation. However, this plane was dropping pamphlets. One of the pamphlets landed in a nearby clearing. Dad picked it up and read it. The pamphlet was a message from General MacArthur giving orders to surrender at Mariveles. My father and Jackson discussed what they should do. If they stayed on the run and were found, they would be shot. They decided to surrender. They had given it their best shot but were unable to find adequate supplies to stay safe and alive. After they wrapped their rifles in a tarp and hung them in the hollow of a tree, they headed for the trail. Dad knew the trail would lead to the highway to Mariveles. As they came out of the jungle they saw an American command car in a clearing.

Outside of the command car stood a very young Japanese soldier. Another soldier inside the car pulled a .45-caliber pistol out of the glove compartment and pointed it at my father and Jackson.

My father said he was worried because he knew the kind of gun the Japanese soldier was brandishing fired very easily. Dad knew that even if the Japanese soldier did not intend to shoot him, it could go off accidentally. Fortunately, the Japanese soldier put the gun away. Then the other soldier said to them, "Where is the whorehouse where you were staying?" Dad and Jackson had not been in such a place but decided to try to lure the Japanese soldiers closer, saying, "Come and we'll show you where it is." Their thoughts of escape had not entirely faded. They thought perhaps they could get the two Japanese soldiers into the jungle and overtake them. Then Jackson and Dad would escape with the command car. The Japanese soldiers either were suspicious or simply decided it was not a good thing to do. Instead, they told Jackson and my father to get into the command car. After they all got in the car, the Japanese drove the car for a distance, then they dropped them off and directed them to head down the road toward Mariveles.[18]

One of the things that intrigued me about my father's retelling of his story was the great disparity in the amount of detail he recalled. In some cases, like this one, he remembered and could say the actual Japanese words of his captors! At other times there were significant periods of time he had virtually no recall of where he was or what transpired. I am quite sure his malaria and the accompanying fever robbed him of his memory. Listening to him, it also became pretty clear that certain events and experiences were burned into his memory and unforgettable.

The two Americans continued on foot to Mariveles. When they got to the surrender point, they saw an ammunition depot on one side of the road with only one Japanese soldier walking around it. As trained soldiers, they found it difficult to give up the fight they had been waging for more than four months.

For a moment they considered trying to overtake the soldier in order to blow up the ammunition. Then they noticed a pile of American uniforms, including shirts, pants, and boots, several feet long and two or three feet high.

---

[18] My father told me the actual words the Japanese soldier said to him at this point, but I was unable to verify the spelling or meaning of what my father said which sounded like "motta goi."

Dad realized they had not seen a single American soldier since leaving their company. He assumed the pile of clothes meant all of them were being shot. Now any thought of trying to escape was gone.

Suddenly more Japanese soldiers appeared. Two of them came quickly toward Dad and Jackson, then kicked and prodded them with their rifle butts back across the road and threw them face down in the rice paddy again near the pile of GI clothes. They lay there the rest of the day. It was during the dry season so the rice paddy was hard and cracked. It wasn't very comfortable, sleep was elusive, and talk had little appeal—they did a lot of thinking and listened to the Japanese soldiers doing their evening rituals. At dusk they were called by the Japanese to a hut across the road, about a half a block away. There, my father recalled that a Japanese officer "counted them out loud, 'Ichi, nee' "[19] (even though there was obviously only two of them) and told them to go back and lie down in the rice paddy.

There they lay all night until dawn the next day. Again they were called to the hut. On their way, they saw two bound American soldiers, a captain and a sergeant, dragged from the hut to the rice paddy. The ropes on the American soldier's hands were cut, the soldiers were ordered to lie down, and both were shot in the back of the head and bayoneted. Witnessing the execution only reinforced my father's belief that the Japanese were summarily executing the surrendering American soldiers.

After being counted, my dad and Jackson were ordered once again to lie down in the rice paddy. Again their sleep that night was fitful, and Dad spent much of the night praying.

The Christian upbringing of his childhood flooded his heart and mind, and he knew ultimately his life was in God's hands. The faith he had embraced as a child, which assured him of a place in heaven when he died, suddenly became very comforting since he assumed the next day would be his last.

---

[19]"One, two" in Japanese.

(Even when my father told this part of his story to my public high school history class in the spring of 1989, he managed to slip in a testimony to his faith. Without mentioning God or Christianity, he told the students when he faced the possibility of death he was not afraid. He said a peace came over him because of what he believed. Then he simply pointed up toward the ceiling.)

As my father lay face down in a rice paddy all night after seeing two other American soldiers executed, his life flashed before his eyes. He said it was as if he were sitting in front of a screen and all the important events and people were pictured in rapid succession. He was barely twenty-one years old, but he knew that he had done some good things and some not-so-good. Prostrate in the dirt, he took the time to confess what he knew to be sin and to pray for forgiveness and mercy. That night, face down in a rice paddy on the Bataan Peninsula, my father prayed that if by some means God would help him survive this rice-paddy execution, he would live the rest of his life for Him.

The next day did not bring my father's or Jackson's death. Instead, without any explanation, they were gathered together with thousands of other prisoners and became part of the Bataan Death March. During the entire time as captives, no food had been given to them, which was a portent of things to come. The rice-paddy incident and a few days without food was just the beginning. Life would flash before my father's eyes again and again over the next three and a half years. Later he learned that the officers who died in the rice paddy had been shot because they were found with pictures of Japanese families on them. They had likely taken the pictures as souvenirs from dead Japanese soldiers.

Cabanatuan was the camp where my father spent most of his time as a prisoner of war. Thousands experienced their lives flashing before their eyes in that camp, and for many it really was the end. At the monument to Cabanatuan in Nueva Ecija, Luzon, a memorial wall stands in tribute to those who died in the camp.

The names are engraved in alphabetical order; last name first, first name, and then rank. When I visited the monument in March 2010, I was looking for my mother's brother Billy, who died while a prisoner there. But I was not thinking very clearly at the moment and so I went to the part of the wall with names beginning with the letter "D" for Davis, which is my maiden name, my father's surname.

There was a William K. Davis, and I took a picture of the name on the wall thinking I had perhaps gotten a picture of my uncle's name. A few minutes later I realized had erroneously been thinking my uncle's last name was Davis. He was Mom's brother, not Dad's. His last name was Brown. So I went back to the wall to the last names beginning with the letter "B." There I found William E. Brown engraved. I took another picture.[20]

Later that evening on the way back to Manila, I was looking through the pictures on my camera. In order to have the photos in a more usable form, each day I would delete photos that were superfluous and put the others into folders on my computer and categorize them for easy retrieval. I intended to delete the picture taken erroneously in the "D" section of the memorial wall. Just as I was about to press the delete button on my camera I glanced at the top of the photo, and partly cut off but still fully readable was the name "Davis, Kenneth E." I was breathless. I thought I had accidentally gotten a picture of my father's name on the wall at Cabanatuan. I was beside myself with joy and at the verge of tears. I was actually shaking, thinking how close I came to losing the photograph. Later, I even blogged about the amazing "accidental photo." I naively thought that looking in the wrong part of the wall for my uncle's name I had found my father's!

---

[20]After returning from my travels I learned from my mother that my uncle's given name was Billie, not William. Consequently, I *still* did not have a picture of my uncle's name from the wall. I contacted our friend Steve Kwiezinski on Corregidor and asked him if he would take a picture of my uncle's name the next time he went to Cabanatuan. To my utter surprise and great joy Steve had already taken a picture of every name on the memorial wall! He immediately emailed me a photo of the part of the wall showing my uncle's name. Brown, Billie E. It took me a while but now I have it. (See photo page 93.)

As I reviewed the facts much later I realized the name was not my father's on the wall. First, it was a memorial wall. Only the names of those who died in the camp are engraved on the wall.

Second, after the name "Davis, Kenneth E." was "Sgt." My dad was a staff sergeant—SSgt. Third, I suddenly remembered my father had told me there was another Kenneth E. Davis, who had died during the war. At one point during the war my grandparents were notified by the United States Army that my dad had died.

They were grief stricken, of course, and wanted more details about where and how he died. After further investigation the Army discovered there were two prisoners at Camp Cabanatuan named Kenneth E. Davis. The name on the wall was Sgt. Kenneth E. Davis from Texas who had died, not SSgt. Kenneth E. Davis from Minnesota. One letter, "S," made the difference between life and death. The *Brainerd Daily Dispatch* featured an article about my dad in the April 7, 1967, issue, which noted, "He was captured by the Japanese and sometime later his parents were notified that he had been killed in action. Several months elapsed before they found that the person who had been killed was a Kenneth Davis from Texas."

I asked my dad's two sisters, Ruthie and Patty, and my mom if they remembered any more of the details about when Dad's parents were notified of his death and how long it was before they were notified that he was still alive. None of them remembered the facts. Ruthie and Patty just remembered being overjoyed when they learned he was alive.

As much as I was disappointed I did not have a photo of Dad's name engraved on the wall at Cabanatuan, I was much more grateful that it was not there. It is tragic that another Kenneth Davis lost his life, but how thankful I am my father survived. Although he came right up to death's door many times, by the grace of God somehow he survived. His life flashed before him many times during his three and a half years as a prisoner of war, but he survived and was given another sixty-four years. I am so grateful for those years. And even more grateful that for almost fifty years I benefitted from being influenced and shaped by his life.

5 A Born Leader

Dad had a strong work ethic and was very determined. He was also a born leader. The combination of these traits was prominent in his work experience. Dad always entered a new job at the bottom. He dropped out of school after the ninth grade. His lack of education likely led employers to conclude that menial labor was all he could handle. But Dad quickly climbed the ladder in every place he worked. He watched and learned and took initiative. As a teenager after the Depression, he joined the CCC (Civilian Conservation Corps) camps, working for three years at the camp in Wilton, Minnesota.[21] He joined the CCC with a friend named Jim Steves (See photo page 90). At the age of seventeen he "supervised the preparation of meals for 180 CCC enlisted personnel. Prepared menus, checked and inspected food supplies for quantity and quality. Directed the work of 10 cooks and kitchen workers."[22] (See document page 106).

After the war Dad did a variety of jobs. He worked for Blau-Gas, Alderman-Maghan Hardware, and Billy Graham Soft Water, all in Brainerd, Minnesota. Then in 1951 my parents bought one hundred sixty acres and a house in Sax, Minnesota, for $5,000. At the time, Dad was making about $100 per month on a dairy farm. Farming did not adequately support his growing family, and by 1955 he was working in the iron ore mines in Eveleth, Minnesota.

---

[21]When I asked my father about his spiritual condition during this period of his life, he said, "I drank some, said my prayers before sleep, and went to a Catholic chapel on Sundays across from the camp." The priest in the chapel was named Taylor. Later Dad would see Father Taylor again when he was in the hospital ward at Camp Cabanatuan in the Philippine Islands.

[22]Army of the United States Honorable Discharge papers, May 13, 1946, p. 3. See document page 106.

In 1964 the mine closed and my father went to work in the taconite mines in Silver Bay, Minnesota.

During his final years on the Mesabi Iron Range in northern Minnesota, Dad worked on one of Jeno Paulucci's research farms.[23] He started out as a general mechanic and farm hand. It was not long before Dad was the foreman overseeing the plant. When the plant was scheduled to move to another location, Mr. Paulucci valued my father's work so much that he offered him the job as the primary manager of his personal properties in Duluth, Minnesota. Dad declined and chose instead to work for the state of Minnesota as a boiler room operator. By the time my father retired from the state of Minnesota after twenty years of service, he was a Grade A, first class, heating and cooling engineer. With only a ninth-grade education, working through one class at a time and one test at a time, his dogged determination and leadership got him to the top of his field.

My father's abilities in leadership and his unswerving tenacity were both useful and strengthened during his fight to survive as a prisoner of war. When he first arrived at Camp O'Donnell, my father was put in charge of burial duty. No training could have ever prepared him for the job. The crew was divided into three task groups: transport of the bodies, digging of the pits, and actual burial of their comrades' bodies. My father described in more detail than usual the horror of the experience. So emaciated and decayed were some of the bodies the skin would slip from the corpses' arms when the POWs tried to lift them into the grave. It was a task almost too cruel to bear when a body had to be rolled or shoveled into the grave.

Dad said that the POWs tried to write down as many of the names and serial numbers as they could, but when caught by the Japanese guards they were punished and their lists were confiscated and destroyed.

---

[23]**Jeno F. Paulucci** (born July 5, 1918) is an American businessman and entrepreneur famous for starting more than seventy companies during his long career. Paulucci's most well-known ventures include his frozen food company, Michelina's Inc., and food products such as Jeno's Pizza Rolls and the Chun King line of Chinese food. He is also involved in charity work, publishing, and public speaking. A self-described "peddler from the Iron Range," Paulucci is closely associated with Northeast Minnesota, where he was born, and known for his candor and colorful public statements.

They nevertheless persisted. The burial crew would memorize as many names and numbers as they could, and when the guards were not looking or were taken away by some other task, the POWs would feverishly record as many names and numbers as possible. My father recalls burying forty to fifty men a day. But it was even worse for the Filipino soldiers and civilians, who had been separated from the Americans and other Allies. They were in a camp across the road and were burying up to two hundred a day. The American POWs knew because they could count the bodies being taken down the road for burial (See painting page 126). Burial duty was not a job anyone wanted. But my father was chosen for the task, and he saw it as an opportunity to try to honor the memory of the men that had been so dishonored by their enemies.

Those men who were not dying were put into work details, one of which was the burial detail. Burial duty detail was one of the worst since it further spread the already rampant diseases. There was no way of determining if a person was dead so it is possible some were buried alive. Burial detail was set up in three groups. The first group of men dug the mass graves without shovels. The graves were anywhere from 10 to 12 feet long and five feet deep.[24]

The second group of men carried the dead in blankets strung over a pole and lined them up along fences. The POWs tried to identify the deceased by getting the men's dog tags, taking one tag with them and shoving the other into the deceased soldiers' mouths, so they could be accounted for. Still, there are some men who were never found and no one knows what happened to them. The POWs on burial detail would then straighten out the decomposing bodies because more fit in the mass graves this way. The third group of men put these dead skeletons into the hole, held them down with a pole, and covered them up with dirt. The ground was so wet from the monsoons that the bodies floated to the surface.[25]

[24]Donald Knox, *Death March* (Orlando: Harcourt Brace, 1981), p. 163. Quoted in Dorothy Cave, *Beyond Courage, Las Cruces, NM: Yucca Tree Press, 1992, p. 218.*

The monsoon season on the Philippines caused wet rains at night and warm humid weather during the day. This made the bodies rise, swell, and stink. When the corpses rose, the men would attempt to cover them up again with grass to show respect for the dead. The bodies had maggots and bugs crawling in and out of them, and the intense heat made the bodies smell. Wild dogs dug up the graves and ate what was left of the rotten corpses.[26]

At Hanawa (or Sendai No. 6) in the north of Japan, my father was also chosen to lead a group of prisoners. Again, he did not know why he was chosen, and there wasn't a whole lot he could do but he gave it his best effort. The group leaders were given the responsibility of distributing any packages that came from the Red Cross or through military channels. Packages rarely came. Or, I should say, packages were rarely distributed. Occasionally the Japanese would allow a few packages to be distributed, and my father took it on as a mission to make sure each one found its way to the man it was intended for. Some POWs offered to buy or even steal packages, and my father admitted the temptation was there for him too. Yet he did his duty with absolute determination. When the Japanese finally surrendered, the abandoned prisoners found stockpiles of packages never distributed by the Japanese.

His responsibilities as a group leader at Hanawa also included arbitrating conflicts between American prisoners. He recalled one time when a fight broke out between two soldiers working with the ore cars deep in the mines. Dad was called to arbitrate.

He said he appealed to the soldier's sense of duty to the other POWs, knowing that any conflict between them would have a negative effect on all of the men. Dad said most of the time the soldiers were very careful about their behavior when they knew the consequences would put the others at risk.

---

[25]Mr. Padilla, curator of Bataan Memorial Military Museum, Santa Fe, New Mexico, December 1999.

[26]Dorothy Cave, *Beyond Courage* (Las Cruces, NM: Yucca Tree Press, 1992), p. 219.

Even when suffering from malnutrition and disease my dad was a leader of others. And his leadership was strengthened in the brutality of these Japanese camps.

I did not experience or ever observe my father as a military-style leader. He didn't often bark orders or demand compliance. He was a servant leader. He led by example. Though he always held positions of authority in all of the churches we attended, he always gave his time and talents in a way that demonstrated leadership was much more than making decisions or exercising power. His desire and ability to help others gave him credibility as a leader. His example of serving others was taken from the example of Christ, who my father knew from studying the Bible. Dad could always recruit people for any task. They liked to be around him and he was a good recruiter because he led them by coming alongside them. He demonstrated his willingness to do the work he was asking others to do. My father's example of leadership has been a constant model for me in my personal and professional life. I learned and experienced the power of working *with* people as opposed to just working people.

Though he had no formal Bible education, his constant studying of Scripture made it clear it was the authoritative guide for all of life. He read it often, quoted it often, and faithfully lived by it. I had the privilege of going to Bible College and eventually to seminary to study the Bible and theology from scholars. I had the privilege of learning from some great professors. But my father was equally influential in my understanding and development as a Christian leader. He was a leader who would come alongside others. He led this way in every church we attended. He came alongside me too. He taught in word and deed what it means to be a leader. He was a born leader, and I learned from the best.

THE EYES OF CAPTIVITY
Oil Painting, 2010

6   Hard Work and Stubborn Determination

After spending three and a half years as a Japanese prisoner of war, in October 1945, while being nursed back to health in Schick General Hospital in Clinton, Iowa, Kenneth Davis, my father, saw her picture. My mother's younger brother Billie had died as a prisoner in Cabanatuan in September, 1942. Her older brother, Alpheus Brown (See lower right photo, page 89), had survived as a POW in Japan. Now he was in the hospital bed next to Dad. Al had a picture of his little sister, Hazel, and he was proudly showing her to Ken (See upper left photo, page 99). Ever the ladies' man, resembling Gene Kelly, Ken cockily declared that he would marry her when he got home. Al was aghast! Over his dead body would Ken get anywhere near his sister! Al had spent way too much time in the hospital bed next to Dad. The guy never shut up! My Uncle Al later told me, "He was so friendly and talkative I thought he was 'queer' or something."[27] Dad and Al were released from Schick General Hospital in Iowa in October, 1945.

Four months later Kenneth Earl Davis married Hazel Irene Brown (See photo page 99), Al's little sister, in a triple wedding. Shortly after Ken and Hazel met, Carl Kramp, also a POW and Bataan survivor started dating Hazel's sister Harriet. Both couples were engaged a month later. "Not wanting to leave Al out of the fun," Harriet introduced him to one of her best friends, Arlene Leibold. Al and Arlene went on their first date December 22. They were engaged three days later. On February 20, 1946, all three couples were married.

The men were in uniform and the women wore identical bridal gowns. The triple wedding took place in the home of William and Olive Brown, Hazel,

---

[27]I don't condone this terminology but it was what my uncle said and the terminology was commonly used at the time.

Harriet, and Al's parents, who lived in Nisswa, Minnesota. Mom said the decision to have a triple wedding was not a difficult one. "We were all such good friends; it just seemed like the thing to do."[28] My father had determination: when he first saw Hazel's picture, he declared he would marry her, and he did.

When Dad set his mind to a task, it was done. The same dogged determination that helped him survive as a POW and got him his bride proved fruitful in every area of his life. After finishing the ninth grade in Pillager, Minnesota, in 1936 Dad never went back to school. Though he was not an educated man, he was extremely intelligent. Whatever he needed to know, he learned. There were few mechanical devices on the planet my father could not fix. He was the paradigmatic jack-of-all-trades. Whether it was taking apart and reassembling a car engine or rehabilitating a toaster, my father was "da man." He could listen to an idling engine and diagnose the problem. He could size up a door frame and produce a specially designed door jamb to match. My father could take one look at a handy device, draw up the plans, and build one of his own. Over the years he acquired enough tools to rival Stanley! I don't remember any other person fixing anything in or around our home. Plumbing, electrical, roofing, additions and renovations, automotive, he could do it all. In our neighborhood and in our church, Dad was the man. If anything needed fixing, he was the first person called.

I found an old trunk in my Auntie Vida's barn attic. It was pretty beat up. At least two of the four wooden straps were sprung. Most of the hardware was missing. The inside was worn and rusted. But I loved it. I had always wanted a trunk. I could see this one had possibilities. My father agreed. He helped me make my mental picture of the trunk become a reality. I do not remember exactly how he did it, but it was done. The wooden straps were re-formed to gently follow the curves of the cover. The missing hardware was replaced. He even cut and sewed new leather straps to go on each end of the trunk. We coated the metal parts with Rustoleum™ and then finished it using antiquing paint. Dad lined it with cedar boards, giving it a genuine look and smell of ages past. My father made it happen.

---

[28]Brad McDermott, "It Was 50 Years Ago," *Brainerd Daily Dispatch*, February 19, 1996, p. 1.

That trunk has followed me through seven states, seventeen cities, and more apartments and houses than I can count. It sits in my family room today, and every person who sees it comments on its beauty. Without any training but with extraordinary fix-it sense, my father made an old trunk from my Auntie Vida's barn the hope chest of my dreams. Every time I touch its wooden straps, open it, and smell its cedar lining I remember my father's dogged determination. When he decided to do something, he always found a way to do it.

The trunk was first renovated between 1973 and 1975, but it was not quite finished. Though Dad had lined the bottom with cedar planks, the cover had never been lined. Now it was 2001 and Dad was coming to visit me in Chicago, and I knew he needed something to do in order to enjoy his visit. I remembered the trunk lid, which I had always wanted to finish. Now was the chance to give him a project and allow me to spend some quality time with him. Dad had been diagnosed with Alzheimer's disease in the fall of 1999, but his fix-it skills remained fully intact even though the disease seemed to be advancing rather quickly. Actually, we determined the disease had likely begun its thievery several years before. In retrospect we could see the signs.

So I purchased the necessary supplies, and when he arrived we set up our project in the garage. We began measuring and cutting and gluing and placing the cedar planks. At one point Dad got frustrated and spoke rather harshly to me. I was taken aback. When I was a dependent child he could at times be gruff and harsh, but since I had left home and become an independent adult, I had never heard a harsh word from him. I didn't take it personally. I knew it was the Alzheimer's, so though I was sad, it didn't make me angry or hurt.

I left the garage to give him some space to work and to relieve my own pain of seeing how Alzheimer's was robbing my father of his personhood. A while later he came in the house, put his arm around me, leaned in to touch his cheek to mine and said, "I am sorry sweetie. I got a little gruff with you out in the garage. I did not realize it was you. Please forgive me."

He didn't know it was me! Alzheimer's was slowly stealing my father away. One moment he knew me and the next he didn't. I was grateful for the chance to spend some time with him no matter what. We finished the trunk, and it's something I will always cherish. In so many ways it represents my father's character. It is solid and beautiful. It knew better days and came close to being forgotten and lost. It was revived and has served so many good purposes in my life. It remains a focal point of my life and home. All these things are true of my father, as well. I hope one of my children will see in it the beauty I do and cherish it when I am gone.

I hope my children will also cherish the record of their grandfather's story as a prisoner of war and how it shaped our family. The original goal of my sabbatical was to travel to the places he described and to "finish" writing his story which I had started so long ago. But as I began to make arrangements for my travel and as I read other accounts of the defenders of Bataan, I discovered a much deeper imprint in my life than the one left merely from the time spent hearing and recording my father's stories. In almost every detail I discovered and in almost every place I visited, I saw the shadows cast on my own life from my father's story. I could now see the distinct imprint of his life as a prisoner of war all through my life.

At the very end of my sabbatical time I traveled with my husband and my brother and his wife to Reno, Nevada, to attend the first annual Descendants of the American Defenders of Bataan and Corregidor (DADBC) Convention. For the last sixty-four years the American Defenders of Bataan and Corregidor (ADBC) have met annually to share camaraderie and to keep their story alive. But the men from this period in history who are still alive are now between the ages of eighty-two and ninety-nine, and many of them can no longer travel. Consequently the descendants of these WWII heroes are attempting to carry on their legacy.

At the convention my brother and I visited with the other children of survivors. It felt similar to many support groups I have attended and led. Though the particulars of each story are very different and the kind of effect it had on each of us ranged widely, the power of our fathers' experiences as prisoners of war resonated in every conversation. Many of our fathers have passed away. Some are still living. But in either case, the power and influence of these fathers on our families is enormous yet easy to underestimate. We all were significantly shaped by our fathers' experiences and our own families are being shaped by them as well.

Dad was determined, but he was human, and so his determination did not always produce the desired result. During the defense of Bataan a Harley-Davidson and a blown up bridge proved to be his match.

It was December 8, 1941, when the American troops in the Philippines were told they had about forty-two hours' "grace" before the Japanese would be in a position to exert serious pressure on them. The nearby Marine base at Olongapo, just down the mountain from Roosevelt Park,[29] toward Subic Bay had been evacuated. Dad's commander instructed him and another soldier, Jackson, to go there to see if there was anything left that might be useful to the base.

Olongapo was a couple of hours away. The road between the two bases had been mined, so they had to be careful. Near Olongapo, the two soldiers found that a small bridge over the river had been blown up. The side supports of the bridge remained intact enough for them to walk across. As they entered the small town near the base, they noticed a gas station on the left, with a like-new Harley-Davidson parked at it. They discovered that the Harley had a full tank of gas, so they decided to take it. What looked like an American officer came out of a nearby building and asked them whether they knew how to ride it. True to Dad's stubborn determination, even though he had never driven a motorcycle before, he replied to the officer, "No, but I'm gonna learn."

---

[29]See footnotes 1 and 9.

Dad left Jackson and took the Harley for a spin. He figured out the throttle, gears, and brakes. He got a little overconfident, though, and was speeding around a corner when he suddenly came upon a sandbag embankment. He had learned how to ride, but not well enough to stop quickly. He overplayed the brakes and went flying over the embankment. God's grace abounds. He got up and was not seriously injured. His determination also abounded. He got back on the Harley and continued to survey the town to see what else might be worth taking. Nothing. He circled back to where he had left Jackson standing.

Now they realized they had a problem in taking the Harley back. The small bridge into Olongapo had already been blown. There was enough left of it to walk across but not enough to drive a motorcycle across. The determination ran deep in my father. He and Jackson found some lumber and began to build a ramp. They had seen motorcycles jumps done in the movies many times over much wider flows of water. Certainly they could jump the Harley over a twenty to thirty foot flow.

I cannot even count the number of times I have thought with this kind of logic. Often when watching a person do some job or feat, I would think to myself, *I could do that!* That kind of thinking actually ended up getting me a job as a restaurant manager in 1984. I had been a waitress and a hostess previously but had never even assisted in management. I had watched the day-to-day operation of several restaurants and believed I could do the job. I made a proposal to a restaurant owner who was looking for a manager, and she took my offer! I ended up successfully managing the mall restaurant to the extent that she decided to purchase another restaurant in the same town and left the first restaurant completely under my care. The only explanation for this kind of brash thinking is a combination of nature and nurture. I inherited the stubborn determination from my father, and I also learned it from watching him.

Back to Dad's problem with the Harley-Davidson in Olongapo. The ramp Jackson and my dad constructed was about four feet high. Jackson was not the daredevil type, so Dad decided to make the jump.

He said he gave the bike gas and took a run at the ramp three times. By his own description, he "chickened out" each time and turned away before hitting the ramp. Frustrated at their inability to get the Harley across the river, they took the spark plugs out of the bike and ran it into the river so the Japanese couldn't use it. Getting to Olongapo and searching for anything useful for the defense of Bataan had taken most of the day. They walked back to their base, hungry. The two men had nothing to eat since they left—food was already scarce and rations were few and far between. In the case of the Harley, my father's determination did not produce the desired result. But when it really mattered—when his life depended on it—his determination saved his life.

My father learned from that Harley much more than just how to ride it. He learned both the possibilities and limits of his determination. The lesson would be repeated over and over again during the next four years, particularly during his three and a half years as a prisoner of war. There were "Harleys" everywhere he turned—things that he was able to use to survive and some he had to learn to let go of in order to survive. His determination was important in both cases. To survive required determination to overcome obstacles but it also required determination not to allow seemingly insurmountable obstacles to have the last say. My father learned a lot from that Harley. And so have I.

I am my father's daughter. I have found Harley's in my life, too. Some I have been able to acquire and use. These experiences have built my confidence. Others I have had to turn away from. Determination can easily become stubbornness. These experiences have taught me humility and have served to teach me to trust God who always finds another way to move me forward.

Certainly POWs died as a result of starvation, disease, and the wounds of war. But other diseased and deprived soldiers survived. Why? I believe, in part, stubborn determination made the difference. Several POWs and children of POWs I have talked with confirm the important part determination plays in survival. And the accounts of Bataan I have read also bear this idea out. The POWs often described the look in the eyes when a soldier had given up. They said you could tell when a soldier was going to die because his eyes grew blank and within a few hours, or a few days at most, he was gone.

But a light shined in the eyes of many who were similarly sick and starving. Their jaws were set. They were determined to not let their captors have the last word. POW survivor Joe Simeroth said he credits one thing—determination—for his survival. He said, "I never once believed I was going to die. When I heard guys say they just couldn't take it anymore, usually within twelve hours they were dead."[30]

In every task, my father exhibited the commitment and determination of a man on a mission. No matter how small or menial the task, he gave it his best. No matter how large and daunting the job, he saw it through to completion. Whatever anyone asked him to do, Dad found the way and means to do it if it was within the realm of possibility. My mother often felt the trait was stubbornness and Lord knows, my father could be stubborn. But that same stubbornness, when directed in a positive way, became sheer determination. He passed the quality on to his children. We are all very determined individuals. We see possibilities in challenges and see challenges as opportunities. Don't tell any of us we cannot do something; it only strengthens our resolve to do it. Stubborn determination is part of the character that was forged in us.

I was the runt of the litter until my baby sister was born when I was thirteen years old. My father used to tell me, "Dynamite comes in small packages." By his example and through his encouragement I grew up to believe that I could do anything I set my mind to. He showed me how my willingness to lead and the size of my determination mattered more than my physical size or resources. Whenever I have come across challenges that appear too big, I remember my dad. He was tested as a prisoner of war for three and a half years and never gave up. How could I give up when I was so free and had so much opportunity?

I inherited my strong determination from my father. I chose to face and I survived challenges because of what I learned from him. He held the deeply rooted belief that we can do anything we set our minds and hearts to do. Whatever challenge faced him, whether it was physical, mechanical, mental, or

---

[30]Joe Simeroth, quoted by Julie Falk, "Memories of the WWII Death March," *Mountain Lake Observer/Advocate*, May 21, 2003, p. 1.

spiritual, I saw the light in his eyes and watched him set his jaw as he attacked whatever was challenging him. By God's grace, my father's determination is one of the things that enabled him to survive the horrors of POW life in the Philippines and Japan. I inherited his strong determination as one of the many gifts I received from my father as a result of being forged by war.

7 A Real Chip off the Old Block

My inheritance of Dad's stubborn determination was clearly evidenced when I was traveling in Southeast Asia to retrace his steps as a POW. My husband and I had already left the Philippines and had visited Japan. Now it was two weeks later and we were in Hong Kong visiting some friends. I had been trying very hard to let go of the fact that while we were in the Philippines I missed two very important places related to his POW experience. I had been trying to simply enjoy and relish what I was able to do and see. I tried not to think about how close I was and yet how I missed such a critical part of my dad's story, but I finally admitted to myself that I couldn't let go. I feared that if I did, I would regret it the rest of my life. I might be able to come back to the Philippines someday, but there was no guarantee. Since I was still in Southeast Asia I knew I had to go back to the Philippines.

Originally, I planned for a man named Steve Kwiezinski, who lives on Corregidor Island and knows the whole Pacific Theater extremely well, to be our guide on Bataan as we retraced my father's footsteps as a POW. Then a member of my church in California offered to host us. She would travel to the Philippines, and she and her nephew, who lives in Manila, would serve as our guides, taking us to the places we wanted to see. We were also scheduled to stay in a vacant house owned by her family in Manila. The parishioner's father and mother live in Manila, and her father, Jaime Marcelo (See drawing page 72), is also a survivor of part of the Death March and was in one of the POW camps my dad was in. I was going to interview him about his experience.[31] Being hosted by the Marcelo family seemed all very good and

---

[31] I did meet and interview Jaime Marcelo, who was a third lieutenant in the 42nd Infantry in the U.S. Army in the Philippines. And I was able to locate his name on the monument at Capas National Monument, where all the Filipino soldiers who served are named on the memorial wall.

appealed to me because of the personal connection. So I cancelled our planned tour guided by Steve Kwiezinski. Then, only two weeks before we were to leave for the Philippines, the matriarch of the family was diagnosed with terminal cancer. All of our plans for Manila had to change. The family needed to concentrate on their mother and her needs.

By this time I could no longer enlist Steve Kwiecinski from Corregidor. He was already booked for another tour. Thankfully, another member of my congregation is a Filipino American, and she said her brother, who lives in Manila, would be happy to help us. He graciously found a good hotel with some discounts for us to stay in, and he agreed to take us to Bataan. I sent him a list of essential places I wanted to visit as well as additional places if there was time. I suggested we stay overnight if needed, and that I would gladly pay all expenses.

A couple of things happened. His wife and two of their friends came along for the ride. They were delightful—really nice people and made the trip a lot of fun. We really enjoyed their company and made new friends as a result. But their various schedules and commitments meant they could not stay overnight, so we had to do all of our touring in one day. We ended up touring from seven in the morning until almost seven at night. The trip back to Manila was another two hours. We had made it to a monument we thought was the terminal point of the Death March and the site of Camp O'Donnell. We had run out of time and did not make it to Cabanatuan, the second POW camp Dad was in and the one he was in the longest. I thought I could live with missing one POW camp. After all, this gentleman had given me so much of his time, gratis, and done his very best. How could I complain?

The next day, my husband and I went to Corregidor and met Steve Kwiecinski who I had originally talked to about being our tour guide for Bataan. We told him about all the places we went to in Bataan. When we were describing the Camp O'Donnell site we visited he said, "That is not the terminal point of the Death March, and it is not the Capas National Monument site where Camp O'Donnell was located!" I was dumbfounded! I had come to accept that I missed seeing the site of the second POW camp my father was in, but now I had learned that I had missed the first camp site as well! How could this have happened?

As I thought about it, I was not totally surprised. We had driven around a lot and had trouble finding the Camp O'Donnell site. Our volunteer guide and driver had to stop several times to ask where the site was located. The area we were driving in had very small and crowded village roads. The monument we saw was actually a small memorial to the Filipinos who were on the Death March. While it was *near* the terminal point of the march, it was *not* where Camp O'Donnell was. The actual location of Camp O'Donnell has a rail boxcar display like the boxcars the prisoners were transported in from San Fernando to Camp O'Donnell (See photo 92). I was just sick when I found this out. We had been within a couple of miles of the Camp O'Donnell site and missed it. The rest of the evening I could not get my mind off of the fact.

My heart ached. I felt sick to my stomach. All these years I had dreamed about making the journey, all the preparation and cost to finally get here and I had missed seeing both POW campsites where my father was imprisoned. Though the gentleman who drove us did his best, he was not familiar enough with the history or the area to get us there. Steve said that it is not easy to find these sites if you do not know the territory.

I had begun to emotionally recover from the fact we had missed the site of the second camp my father was in, Cabanatuan, but now I learned I had also missed the site of the first camp, Camp O'Donnell. I could hardly believe it! We had missed both POW campsites! The disappointment was hard to accept after coming all the way, spending all the money and investing so much emotional energy. I tried to arrange a way to go back to Bataan two days later on Thursday but could not pull it off, and Drew and I left for Tokyo on Friday. Oh, how my heart ached.

I tried hard. I really did. I tried to apply the stubborn determination and optimism I had learned from my father. I was determined to put on the best face and talk myself into it being okay. For ten days I put my best face forward. But the determination I had inherited from my father was pushing in two different directions. One direction was to accept what was. The other was the resolve to see those places I had come to see but had missed.

Finally, my resolve to see the camps where my father had been a prisoner of war won out. Now in Hong Kong, I decided to find a way to go back to the Philippine Islands. If I could find a reasonably priced flight and a reliable guide I could afford, I would go back. I thought to myself, *I must touch the ground, I must see the places, I must have a first-hand experience of the history of these two prisoner of war camps my father survived. I must go back!*

I went online and checked out the flights. There were reasonable flights from Hong Kong to Manila available in the short window of time I had. I contacted Steve Kwiecinski on Corregidor to see if he could arrange an affordable and reliable driver and car on such short notice. I had just two days to pull the return trip off without totally upsetting the remaining itinerary I had ahead of me. I was beside myself with excitement when all the pieces fell into place. I booked a flight online and Steve was able to secure an experienced driver and guide who had taken him to these camps before. I was going back to see O'Donnell and Cabanatuan! I could not miss the perhaps once-in-a-lifetime opportunity. I hardly slept at all the night before I returned.

When I think back on it now, after seeing what I saw by returning, I can't imagine having come home without seeing the O'Donnell and Cabanatuan sites. I'm so very grateful that my father's stubborn determination was passed down to me. I am also grateful that my husband, though he could not return with me, encouraged me to go back. I would have missed so much. The amazing journey I was able to take would not have been complete without the return to Bataan.

My return to Bataan led to a lot more tears. They just came. The minute I saw the places and touched the earth and the significant parts of the monuments, the tears came. I know the emotion was in part due to the recent loss of my father in 2006, though Alzheimer's had taken him from us about three years before that. I was crying for many reasons; chief among them was the loss of his life mixed with the emotion of retracing his steps. The tears also came as a result of a deeper understanding of the enormity of suffering and loss represented by these places. I was contemplating my dad's experience multiplied by hundreds of thousands all over the world during WWII.

Steven, my driver, picked me up at the hotel in Manila at 7:30 a.m. He proved to be a very capable and empathetic guide. He knew exactly where we were going and wasted no time in getting there. But once there, he was extremely patient and supportive. Somehow he knew how important and emotional the journey was for me. He took the time to stop and show me several other smaller WWII memorials on our tour that day. Each place we visited, he allowed as much time as I needed to see the site. He always remained at a distance to allow me privacy but was always available if I was ready to go. Each time I headed back to the car, Steven would first start the car and begin to cool it down, and then he would get out and open the car door for me to get in. On one occasion when the tears were more abundant, he brought me a tissue from the car and reassured me that I could take as much time as I needed.

Later, on our way back to Manila, I learned the day he was guiding me was his daughter's sixteenth birthday. They were having a party for her that night. In spite of this important event in his life, never once during that day did he try to hurry me even though we did not return to Manila until 7 p.m., and Steven had another hour to drive home. I could not have had a more capable and kind guide for my return to the Philippines. As we drove back to Manila, my heart was singing. What a day this had been! How grateful I was for the time, resources, and determination to return. In so many ways my father *was* with me on that day.

From childhood I have experienced this stubborn determination. Any hint of challenge could set me off on a mission to prove the thing was doable. Time and again I would find myself in the middle of a seemingly insurmountable problem and wonder, *how did I get myself into this?* In the early 1970s it was recycling that got me going. Long before the local governments took on the task of recycling newsprint, I led my little high school in southern Minnesota to establish a recycling program. I was told the task was too hard for high school students.

We started the program from scratch. We found an empty building at the local county fair property and lobbied for its free use. We set up a pick-up and drop-off schedule. We successfully found donated trucks and volunteer drivers (my dad was one of them, of course) to deliver our newsprint collection to our contracted recycler one hundred miles away. I remember standing in the middle of our recycling building filled with paper and wondering, *how did I get myself into this?* My little recycling project had grown into a full-blown affair requiring hundreds of volunteers, thousands of hours, and complex scheduling and resourcing arrangements.

I find myself presently in a job that common sense would say was way beyond my experience and ability. Eight years ago I accepted the call as the pastor of a mainline church that had been in decline for almost thirty years. The building was in considerable disrepair. The organizational structure had deteriorated into several small interest groups. The congregation was predominantly white and over seventy-five in a community that now was sixty percent Latino, whose average age was thirty-six. It had seen three interim pastors and a called pastor that lasted a mere three years. I had been an associate pastor in a larger, mostly Anglo, mainline church for seven years. What made me think that I could take this church and help to transform it?

Stubborn determination, which I inherited from my father, and a good measure of positive thinking and unrepentant optimism all came together. Along with a sense of call from God and a corresponding affirmation of others around me, these things brought me to this challenging vocational place. My decision to take such a call was significantly shaped by my father's influence on me. Hard work and stubborn determination used by the good Lord won the day. Today the congregation is thriving as a multicultural community. Now more than fifty percent of those who attend are not Anglo. The congregation is also more diverse socioeconomically and generationally. It is an unusual example of the rich diversity of the people of God. The transformation of my congregation is the result of the work of my heavenly Father, of course. But my earthly father also contributed through his deep and lasting imprint in my life.

JAIME MARCELO
Pencil Drawing, 2010

8 Pie Crusts and Block Letters

I got married very young, two months short of twenty. I had spent most of my growing years with my dad in the garage or the barn or on a tractor out in the field. Then when I was a teenager I was very active in my school and community. I got my first part-time job when I was only thirteen. I worked from that time all through high school. As a result I never really learned how to cook. When I got married I think I knew how to boil hot dogs and heat a can of soup. I remember making chocolate chip cookies using the recipe on the back of the Nestle's™ semi-sweet chocolate chip bag. But I don't remember spending any other time in the kitchen learning how to cook or bake. Fortunately, my husband wasn't a demanding person and had grown up on a pretty simple meal plan. I learned the basics quickly. He often helped with meals. We did just fine.

In the culinary department I do have a reputation for exceptional quality with one thing—pie crusts. I never buy ready-made crusts. I always make my pie crusts from scratch. They are thin, flakey and sweet. The amazing thing about this skill is, contrary to what you might expect, my father taught me to make pie crusts! I don't remember when it was or why he, rather than my mother, taught me, but it definitely was my dad. The rough and tough man, who was stronger than a horse and who couldn't bend a couple of his fingers due to a table-saw injury, showed me how to cut in the Crisco™ and shape and roll out the dough. He taught me how to use the right amount of flour on the rolling surface and the rolling pin. He showed me how to gently pull the crust from the rolling surface and carefully lay it in the pie tin. And to top it off, Dad taught me how to beautifully and uniformly flute the edges of the pie crust.

I know the ability to make wonderful pie crusts did not come from his years as a prisoner of war. It likely came from his years working as a cook in the Civilian Conservation Corps, which was a precursor to his enlistment in the Army.[32] From about 1936 to 1939 he worked as a cook in the CCC camp in Wilton, Minnesota. According to his military records he supervised others as well. He was just a teenager at the time and yet was already leading others in very important ways.

My father also taught me how to draw and cut out uniform block letters. I learned to make them any size I needed, very small or very large. He also taught me how to make shaded block letters, explaining how to imagine a light shining on the letters. The way I shaded the letters depended on where the light was coming from. He put some objects on the table and used a flashlight to show me how different shadows were created on the objects depending on the direction of the light. Then he helped me draw the block letters and showed me how to use shading to make them three-dimensional. At the time I did not know where he learned to make these letters. Now I know it was at least in part from his training as a regimental draftsman, but I think he also had some innate artistic ability. His mechanical hands and artistic eye allowed him to create all sorts of gadgets and gizmos, including fancy lettering.

I have used this making-letters skill often. When I was growing up I used it in projects and posters for school; I gained a reputation for being able to make fancy letters and cool school projects. In the rough and tough tumble of a small country school where I could not begin to compete in material possessions or physical beauty, an artistic skill my father passed on to me gave me a real sense of significance. It made me feel special when I most often felt common and unnoticed. My third-grade teacher, Mrs. Saline, let me make bulletin board displays for our classroom. When the other students were working on other art projects I got to design and put up these displays.

Later, when I became a social studies teacher, it came in very handy for classroom displays and bulletin boards of my own. The skill has also been useful in every job I have had in the church.

---

[32]See page 131..

Ministry is often mentally and emotionally taxing, so it is a great relief on occasion to simply make something with my hands and have it be appreciated by others.

Trying to do for others what my father did for me, I have often helped other children and students make simple letters become three-dimensional by shading. And I have shown students and adults working on bulletin boards how to quickly make uniform letters for display using the method my father taught me.

These are just a couple more of the memories I have of my father's imprint in my life. I am not much of a cook, but my pies rarely fail. And the excellent crust always reminds me of him. And when I make block letters and shade them for artistic purposes, I always get positive feedback. Of course, I think of my dad and am thankful for the myriad ways he left his mark in my life. Pie crust and block letters. Simple things. Yet they are profound reminders for me of his influence on my life.

9 A Little Help from My Friends

On the Bataan Death March the Japanese soldiers in charge were very predictable. The prisoners usually were not allowed to help each other. On occasion healthier men were allowed to help weaker soldiers by supporting them, one under each arm. More often, if a man could not walk and fell, he was left to die or was shot or bayoneted. And most of the time, when others tried to help, they were kicked and hit with the butt of a rifle until they stopped helping, or they too were often killed. Filipino peasants stood helplessly along the way as they watched the sick and starving men march by. Some tried to help by giving food and water to the prisoners, but if they were caught, they too were punished or killed. Word spread fast, so few tried to help.

My dad recalled two older men handing out sugar lumps the size of hamburgers. When a Japanese soldier saw them he yelled, "Dami, dami," which means "No good, no good." The Filipino men were scared and ran into the nearby rice paddy only to be chased by the soldiers and killed. There was no giving aid to the weak and dying. The poem of Lt. Henry G. Lee conveys it all.

> So you are dead. The easy words contain
> No sense of loss, no sorrow, no despair.
> Thus hunger, thirst, fatigue, combine to drain
> All feeling from our hearts. The endless glare,
> The brutal heat, anesthetize the mind.
> I cannot mourn you now. I lift my load,
> The suffering column moves. I leave behind
> Only another corpse, beside the road.[33]

---

[33]Lt. Henry G. Lee, quoted in Knox, "Death March"

Although most of the Japanese captors tried everything in their power to stop POWs from helping one another, their efforts were not always successful—at least after the Death March. From camps and the work details there are stories of POWs helping each other with or without the approval of the Japanese guards. My father conveyed some of these stories.

From the POW camp Cabanatuan my father volunteered for a detail sent to Limay to do bridge repair. At first prisoners volunteered for these work details because they were under the impression that they would be given more to eat in order to sustain their work. However, work details did not automatically mean better food. Often the rations were no different even though the work was more demanding. My father said men also volunteered just to escape the boredom of the camps.

On his Limay detail he credited his work crew with saving his life. Anyone caught not working was shot by the Japanese guards. Unfortunately, my father was seriously ill from malaria. Usually between 9 a.m. and 1 p.m. he would pass out from malarial fever. At first when he passed out his friends would hide him behind a bush or in the tall grass until he came to. At some point a guard found him and was preparing to shoot him, but his crew acted to protect him. Three of the men from his crew bargained with the guard, guaranteeing that they would do as much work as four men if the guard would look the other way when my father passed out. On that day, thank God, the Japanese guard agreed to the deal. He allowed the crew to help their crewmate. My father's friends on the crew worked extra hard and my dad's life was spared.

On another occasion my father was the one who gave the help. When Jackson and my father were on their way to surrender, they found a bottle of quinine in a ditch. They kept it knowing it was malaria medicine. They saw so many sick soldiers at the beginning of the Death March they gave it all away. Later, when my father needed quinine he had none left.

Sometimes help came in the form of information. My dad's dysentery got bad enough he was sent to the hospital area of the camp at Cabanatuan. Being sent to the "hospital area" didn't mean he was given medical attention.

It simply meant he wouldn't be sent out on any work details. Many of the POWs called it the "death ward" or "zero ward" because anyone sent there had about a zero chance of coming out alive. Dad's dysentery was so severe he began passing the lining of his stomach. Another POW remembered his mother saying that eating charcoal would prevent more damage. My father and the other POW were able to find a burned building in the camp, and they ate the charcoal off the burned building to prevent further harm to their stomachs.[34]

Sometimes the help came at great sacrifice. The prisoners in the Japanese camps were organized into work details of ten men. Japanese camp policy dictated if any one of a group of ten escaped the other nine would be killed.[35] However, through bribes some Japanese guards would allow a couple of American soldiers to go out of the camp to get contraband—mostly food—as long as they gave some of it to the guards. My father remembered during one such contraband run in Cabanatuan there was a changing of the guards. The new guards did not tolerate such arrangements. The two Americans on the outside could not return without facing severe punishment, so they decided to escape. But they remembered the policy and changed their minds and returned to the camp. When they turned themselves in, the Japanese guards gave them each some water and a cigarette. After they had smoked the cigarettes, the guards had them dig their own graves. The soldiers were shot and stuck with the bayonets, and shoved into their graves. My father credited these two American soldiers with honor and courage that saved eighteen lives.

My father told me about another soldier in his group who had witnessed the policy applied when one prisoner escaped and did not return. The nine men in his group were executed.

---

[34]Michael Norman and Elizabeth N. Norman, *Tears in the Darkness* (New York: Farrar, Straus, Girraux, 2009), p. 241, describes doctors giving charcoal from the kitchens to dysentery patients to try to control diarrhea.

[35]Manny Lawton, *Some Survived* (Chapel Hill, NC: Algonquin Books, 2004), p.72; and Norman and Norman, *Tears in the Darkness*, p. 223.

The soldier described in some detail what happened. The nine men were lined up and given water. Then a young Japanese soldier with a machine gun shot them one by one until the last one was on his knees crying out for a drink of water. The Japanese soldier shot him, too.

The Japanese version of group punishment played out another time in northeast Japan. Dad said three days after he was at the Osarizawa mine at Hanawa, a Japanese commander found his uniform missing. The prisoners were told no one would get food until the thief confessed. No one would admit guilt. So, five or six prisoners decided to gamble with a deck of cards. They all agreed to draw cards and the low man would take the rap. Once again, honor and courage was displayed. The low man was taken by an American officer to the Japanese officer and made a false confession. But here the story takes a humorous and hopeful turn.

The American officer decided to plead insanity for the confessing soldier. He told the Japanese officer the soldier was crazy and did not know what he was doing. And the soldier played the part, acting like a raving lunatic. The Japanese officer and his accompanying soldiers were amused and laughed and laughed. So enamored were they with the crazy American soldier they decided to make him a "toban." A toban shined and polished the shoes of the Japanese soldiers. But the toban also got fed better than any other prisoners in the camp! A little honor and courage sprinkled with a little humor paid off. My dad said later the stolen uniform was found in the straddle trenches (latrines), but they never found out who put it there.

Humor was a friend more than once during my father's imprisonment. At one of the camps, and I do not remember which one it was, the Japanese guards made it clear they loved Hollywood stars. They would go around the camp saying they were Kirk Douglas or Cary Grant. They wanted to know more names of Hollywood stars. So the American POWs obliged them, giving them the names of Donald Duck, Mickey Mouse, and Yogi Bear.

These Japanese guards began referring to themselves as Donald Duck or Mickey Mouse! The POWs were delighted. Oh, the simple ways one can conquer an enemy! I have since read the accounts of other POW's who tell of similar antics.[36] These small moments of comic relief from the suffering and pain of captivity were friends indeed! The Beatles song is absolutely right; "I get by with a little help from my friends."

---

[36]In 2010 I had a conversation with Steve Kwiecinski, whose father was also at Cabanatuan. Steve said his father told him the same story.

WHERE MEN ONCE STARVED
Oil Painting, 2010

10 I think he was a Good Man

One of the greatest lessons my father taught me was about prejudice and stereotypes. He taught by the stories he told and also by the way he lived his life. The story I have recounted about the young Japanese couple that came to our house is perhaps one of the most powerful lessons he gave me (See "Mr. Hospitality," chapter 11). But some stories from his days as a prisoner of war also reveal my father's unprejudiced treatment of others.

After a short period of time in the hospital ward at Cabanatuan my dad's health improved enough to again volunteer for a work detail, this time at Clark Field. He was there about a month digging rocks that the Japanese crushed and used to repair the air fields, but his dysentery flared up again. Dad was sent to Bilibid (See photo page 94), a Filipino criminal prison in Manila where twelve cells were fenced off for POWs with dysentery. They were allowed to bathe at an outside faucet, but were not allowed in the "shower" after 4 p.m. My father recalled a man at Bilibid named Griffin received a first aid package and letter from his girlfriend. This parcel was the first delivered package or letter Dad saw during his imprisonment. He thinks Griffin was so preoccupied with his mail he lost track of time and ended up in the shower after 4 p.m. A Japanese guard on the wall, who my father said was crazy and dying from gonorrhea, jumped down from the wall and said in Japanese, "Today I die, and so do you." With that he shot Griffin in the chest. He then put the gun to his neck and pulled the trigger, blowing off his chin. Doctors were summoned for both, but they were unable to save Griffin.[37]

---

[37]In the taped interview with Harold Spooner in 1993, my father expressed remorse that he had not tried or been able to contact Griffin's girlfriend after the war. He simply said, "I should have got ahold of her."

When I asked Dad why doctors were summoned in this case, since the Japanese had such a blatant disregard for human life and there was a clear policy against being in the showers after 4 p.m., he said the wall guard was not authorized to execute Griffin. He also said the attempt to save Griffin's life was because of the Japanese commander in charge. Then Dad said something totally unexpected in reference to the Japanese commander: "I think he was a good man." In the middle of his three and a half years of imprisonment my father had already seen enough brutality and inhumanity from the Japanese to cause anyone to conclude that all Japanese soldiers were monsters. Others have developed a deep prejudice and further concluded that all Japanese people were bad. Not my father. In the midst of horrors few survived my father could still see good in people—even in his enemies.

During my visit to the Philippine Islands in the spring of 2010 my husband and I also had the chance to visit the site of the old Bilibid prison. Before the war began a new prison was being built south of the city to replace Bilibid. Shortly after the war the prisoners were transferred to the new prison. But Old Bilibid, as it has come to be known, remains and today is the Manila City Jail (See photo page 94). With picture in hand I was determined to see where my father was brought when he was near death as a POW. It is not an easy place to find and it is an even more difficult place to see. The neighborhood around the jail is very dangerous and not the kind of place we would have been able to go to on our own. However, our driver amazed us in how he navigated the narrow streets and knew just where to go to get to the main entrance. We never would have found it on our own.

We could not see the front façade that was in the picture I had of Old Bilibid Prison (See photo page 94). Eduardo, our driver, tried to talk the front entrance guard into letting us go inside the jail to see if perhaps the old façade was now on the inside of the jail. Eduardo was as determined as I was. He explained to the guard why I was visiting the site. Could we go inside just for a quick look? The answer was no. He tried bargaining with the guard and offered him some cash. The answer was still no. When the guard finally explained that he could lose his job if he were caught letting us inside, Eduardo gave up. He explained to me later that he did not want to jeopardize the guard's job; after all, the guard told Eduardo he had three children at home.

However, Eduardo was determined to get us a better look at the place. We wound our way through the surrounding streets and buildings to a pedestrian walkway about two stories above and directly over the jail. From here we could see the inner part of the jail. The center tower stood just as it was during the war with the "barracks" radiating out from the center tower.

Once again I had such an incredible sense of being where my dad was. The facility still held prisoners, but these prisoners are criminals. There were criminals in Bilibid when my father was there, but the Japanese had cordoned off part of the prison for very ill POWs. Once again, I was on the outside looking in, where my father had been on the inside looking out. In my conversations with Dad he often spoke about Bilibid. I was so grateful to be there, even if I was on the outside.

Bilibid was not the only time during my father's imprisonment that he recognized a good person. When he was working in the copper mines in northern Japan he had another encounter with a Japanese soldier who demonstrated some goodness. One day when Dad was working, dumping carts of extracted copper into the gravity shoot and recording the amounts, a young Japanese soldier, who my dad described as "a kid with a gun," said to my dad in Japanese, "Pretty soon no war and I will come to your house." My dad said that he replied, "You do and I'll cut your head off." The young guard came at Dad with his bayonet, but a Japanese commander—a "honcho," as my father called him—came around the corner just as the guard charged him. The commander stopped the young soldier and saved my dad's life. The young Japanese soldier was reprimanded. Regarding that commander my father said once again, "I think he was a good man."

My father was not alone in recognizing good men among his enemies. In 2010 I had the privilege of meeting a Japanese man named Paul Fukuda (See photo page 96). Another Presbyterian pastor put me in contact with Paul, who helped my husband and me when we visited Japan during my sabbatical.

After hearing a little about my father's story and in preparation for our arrival in Tokyo, he explained to me why he was very interested in assisting us. In an email he wrote:

> My father, who passed away in 1987, was a geologist specializing in rare-metal-containing ores such as molybdenum and manganese, which were used for the production of the fighter plane engines' parts. During the war, he was assigned to Hokkaido, further north from Sendai, at a mine where ores were excavated. My father had to supervise Korean laborers who had been forced to leave their hometowns to engage in the "State Essential Industries," and American POWs, both working in the mine. Immediately after the war, he was "purged" from public positions by the General Headquarters of Occupation Military Government (for the reason of having been in the position of employing forced laborers and POWs) and tentatively retired in a small village located between Sendai and Tokyo.

> In November of 1945 my father received a telegram from the head of the Korean workers, whom he had supervised until the Surrender Day, asking him to come, a few days later in the middle of the night, to Japan Railways' Sukagawa Station on the Tohoku Trunk Line and wait for such and such a train. Sukagawa Station was the nearest to where our family lived together with my father. It connected northern cities and villages with Tokyo. Wondering what might develop at the station, my father decided to comply with that request.

> To this day I remember that cold November night when my father gave me, eight years old at the time, a ride on the back of a bicycle to travel 20 kilometers to the town of Sukagawa. We waited at the station for a long time, as trains never ran on time in those days on account of air-raid-damaged equipment, coal shortages, etc. At long last a steam-locomotive-pulled train came into the station premises. It was an express train that would not normally make a stop at a small town station like Sukagawa. But, it did stop. The train carried many, many Koreans going back to their homeland on the peninsula across the water from Kyushu, the southwestern end of Japan.

They had been brought from their own towns and villages to engage in the War Essential Industries in the northern regions of Japan and now were liberated by the Occupation Administration. The workers at the mine where my father had been posted were among those passengers, and they forced the locomotive engineer and fireman to stop the train. About two dozen of those workers came down to the track and offered to my father bags of rice, corn and beans, and packages containing butter and sugar, saying, "Thank you Shocho-san [honorable manager] for having been so kind to us during those hard days. We are going home now but had to say goodbye and thank you to you. Feed your family with our gift." They got back on the coach and the train slowly pulled out of the Sukagawa Station. My father was waving his arms in his full might until the train completely disappeared into the twilight of the dawn.[38]

Paul Fukuda's father was a Japanese scientist employed by the "War Essential Industries" of the Japanese government that waged war on America and imprisoned my father for three and a half years. But I know my father would have agreed with the Korean workers in saying, "He was a good man."

I realize that not every WWII veteran or POW has or had this perspective, but I have talked too many who did. And I have talked to other descendants of WWII POWs who said they also learned the same lesson from their fathers. What human history teaches us—if we will learn—is that every race and nation has good people and bad people. When we experience evil on a very personal level at the hands of another human being, we are tempted to generalize that same evil to the entire group or race represented by that person. Transferring the evil of one to the whole is called prejudice or stereotyping. Given all the evil my father experienced and all the suffering he endured, if any human being had a justifiable cause for prejudice, he did. Knowing how he reacted is why the lesson is so powerful.

---

[38]Paul Fukuda, email to Candie Blankman dated January 29, 2010. Text is slightly edited for clarity.

My father, and many like him, rose above the evil they suffered and chose to see the good in people, regardless of race or national allegiance. Even in his darkest days my father could see the good in those around him. I was imprinted with his view of the world. I am a bit naive and am often taken advantage of as a result. I am often criticized for having this view of people and life. But I am my father's child *and* my Father's child. Both of these, my heavenly Father and my earthly father, have taught me to err on the side of hope and optimism. So, I do. I know many people in the world differ with me on all sorts of issues and debates and convictions and political views. In spite of these differences I try to see the good in them and to think they too might be good people.

Ken (3rd from left) with his seven brothers.

Ken before enlistment in 1940.   Alpheus and Billie Brown in 1940.

CCC camp mess hall where Ken worked.

Coworker Jim Steves at CCC camp.

First line of defense,
Bataan Peninsula.

View of Mt. Mariveles
from the Death March.

The Bataan Death March.

Box car like the ones that transported POWs from San Fernando to Capas.

POWs arriving at Camp O'Donnell, April 1942.

Memorial cross at Capas National Shrine.

Cabanatuan Monument.

The name of Ken's brother-in-law Billie on the Cabanatuan Memorial Wall.

Another Kenneth E. Davis that died at Camp O'Donnell.

Bilibid Prison entrance in 1944.

Entrance to Manila City Jail today, formerly Bilibid Prison.

Jail central tower is the same today as in 1944.

Manila harbor pier, Noto Maru departure point.

Hell Ship, painting by Ben Steele.

The Hell Ship Noto Maru.

View of mountains from the train to Hanawa.

Candie and her husband Drew at the entrance to Hanawa mine.

Paul Fukuda and Candie.

Nori Nagasawa and Candie.

Gravestone for POWs who died in the Hanawa mine.

Military aerial photo of supply drop to Hanawa Sendai #6, August 1945.
Notice parachute in upper right corner of photo.

Hazel Brown in 1942.

Ken and Hazel before their wedding, February 1946.

Ken and Hazel's triple wedding, February 20, 1946.

Ken with his five children at the VA hospital in Tomah, WI.

Ken's gravestone at Fort Snelling National Cemetery.

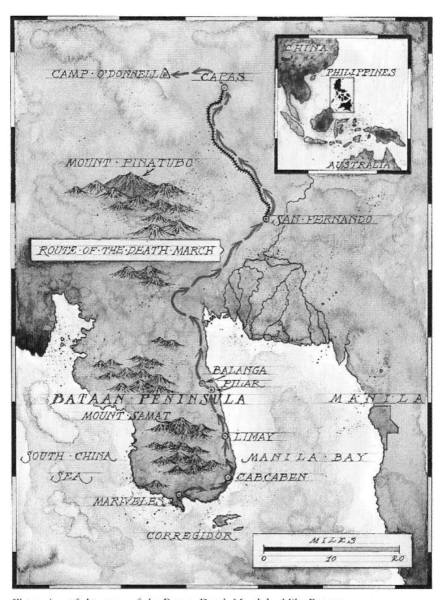

Illustration of the route of the Bataan Death March by Mike Reagan.

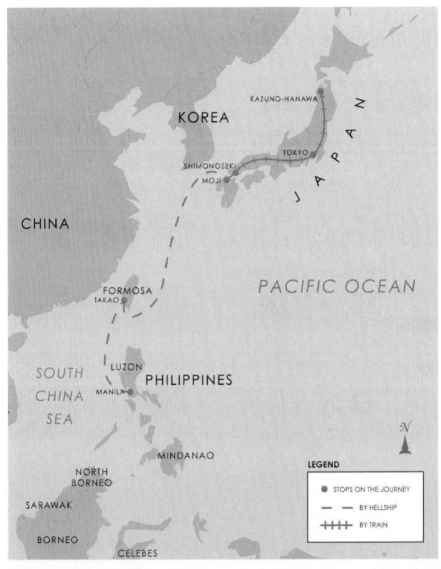

Ken's journey through WWII.

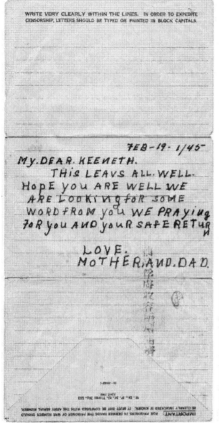

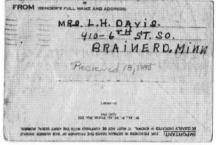

Telegram from Ken's mother in 1945.

Clipping from the Lake Country Echo, May 1992. Ken and Hazel at the naming of Nisswa legion post after Billie Brown, Hazel's brother who died at Cabanatuan in 1942.

Clipping from the Brainerd Dispatch of Ken placing a wreath at the Bataan Memorial in Brainerd, Minnesota.

Clipping from the Brainerd Dispatch, April 1998, of Ken at the Fall of Bataan Memorial Ceremony in Brainerd Minnesota.

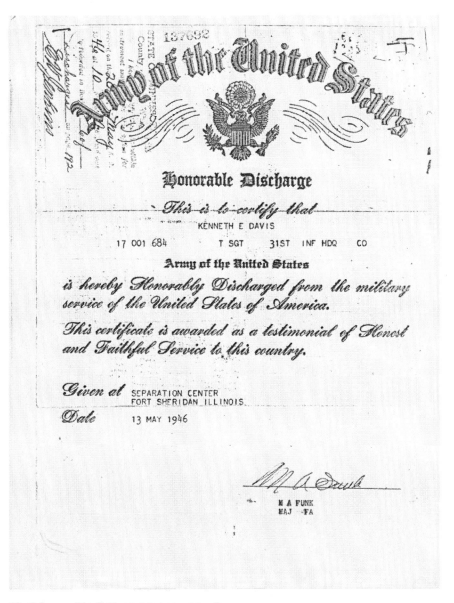

Ken's honorable discharge papers - page 2.

MILITARY EDUCATION

14. NAME OR TYPE OF SCHOOL—COURSE OR CURRICULUM—DURATION—DESCRIPTION

None

CIVILIAN EDUCATION

15. HIGHEST GRADE COMPLETED	16. DEGREES OR DIPLOMAS	17. YEAR LEFT SCHOOL	OTHER TRAINING OR SCHOOLING	
			20. COURSE—NAME AND ADDRESS OF SCHOOL—DATE	21. DURATION
1 yr H.S.	None	1936		
18. NAME AND ADDRESS OF LAST SCHOOL ATTENDED			None	
Pilleger H.S., Minnesota				
19. MAJOR COURSES OF STUDY				
Academic				

CIVILIAN OCCUPATIONS

22. TITLE—NAME AND ADDRESS OF EMPLOYER—INCLUSIVE DATES—DESCRIPTION

COOK, COMBINATION

C.C.C. Camp Bemidji, Minnesota, from 1938 to 1939. Supervised the preparation of meals for 180 C.C.C. enlisted personnel. Prepared menus, checked and inspected food supplies for quantity and quality. Directed the work of 10 cooks and kitchen workers.

ADDITIONAL INFORMATION

23. REMARKS

None

24. SIGNATURE OF PERSON BEING SEPARATED	25. SIGNATURE OF SEPARATION CLASSIFICATION OFFICER	26. NAME OF OFFICER (Typed or Stamped)
		GORDON J MOTT MAJ AC

Ken's honorable discharge papers - page 3.

ENLISTED RECORD AND REPORT OF SEPARATION
HONORABLE DISCHARGE

1. LAST NAME - FIRST NAME - MIDDLE INITIAL	2. ARMY SERIAL NO.	3. GRADE	4. ARM OR SERVICE	5. COMPONENT
DAVIS KENNETH F	17 001 684	T SGT	INF	AUS

6. ORGANIZATION	7. DATE OF SEPARATION	8. PLACE OF SEPARATION
31ST INF HDQ CO	13 MAY 46	SEPARATION CENTER FORT SHERIDAN ILLINOIS

9. PERMANENT ADDRESS FOR MAILING PURPOSES	10. DATE OF BIRTH	11. PLACE OF BIRTH
BOX 252 LAKE HUBERT MINN	24 MAR 1921	BARROWS MINN

12. ADDRESS FROM WHICH EMPLOYMENT WILL BE SOUGHT	13. COLOR EYES	14. COLOR HAIR	15. HEIGHT	16. WEIGHT	17. NO DEPEND.
SEE # 9	BRO	BRO	5-6½	180 LBS.	0

18. RACE	19.	MARITAL STATUS	20. U.S. CITIZEN	21. CIVILIAN OCCUPATION AND NO.
WHITE NEGRO OTHER (specify)	SINGLE MARRIED OTHER (specify)	X	YES NO	COOK COMBINATION 2 26 05

MILITARY HISTORY

22. DATE OF INDUCTION	23. DATE OF ENLISTMENT	24. DATE OF ENTRY INTO ACTIVE SERVICE	25. PLACE OF ENTRY INTO SERVICE
	1 SEPT 40	1 SEP 40	FT SNELLING MINN

SELECTIVE SERVICE DATA	27. LOCAL S.S. BOARD NO.	28. COUNTY AND STATE	29. HOME ADDRESS AT TIME OF ENTRY INTO SERVICE
REGISTERED YES X NO			410 6TH ST BRAINED MINN

30. MILITARY OCCUPATIONAL SPECIALTY AND NO.	31. MILITARY QUALIFICATION AND DATE (i.e., infantry, aviation and marksmanship badges, etc.)
DRAFTSMAN 070	COMBAT INFANTRYMAN BADGE

32. BATTLES AND CAMPAIGNS
PHILIPPINE ISLANDS   SOUTHERN PHILIPPINES

33. DECORATIONS AND CITATIONS
VICTORY MEDAL   AMERICAN THEATER RIBBON   ASIATIC PACIFIC THEATER RIBBON WITH 2 BRONZE BATTLE STARS   9 OVERSEAS SERVICE BARS   1 SERVICE STRIPE   GOOD CONDUCT MEDAL

34. WOUNDS RECEIVED IN ACTION
NONE

35. LATEST IMMUNIZATION DATES				36.	SERVICE OUTSIDE CONTINENTAL U.S. AND RETURN		
SMALLPOX	TYPHOID	TETANUS	OTHER (specify)	DATE OF DEPARTURE	DESTINATION	DATE OF ARRIVAL	
SEP 45	SEP 45	NOV 45	FLU NOV 45	17 NOV 40	PTO	5 DEC 40	

37.	TOTAL LENGTH OF SERVICE					38. HIGHEST GRADE HELD	16 OCT 45	USA	27 OCT 45
CONTINENTAL SERVICE			FOREIGN SERVICE						
YEARS	MONTHS	DAYS	YEARS	MONTHS	DAYS	T/ SGT			
0	8	26	4	11	11				

39. PRIOR SERVICE
NONE

40. REASON AND AUTHORITY FOR SEPARATION
SEC 1 WD CIR 94 DTD 20 MAR 46

41. SERVICE SCHOOLS ATTENDED
NONE

PAY DATA

42. LONGEVITY FOR PAY PURPOSES	43.	44. MUSTERING OUT PAY		45. SOLDIER DEPOSITS	46. TRAVEL PAY	47. TOTAL AMOUNT, NAME OF DISBURSING OFFICER
YEARS MONTHS DAYS 5 8 27	TOTAL 300	THIS PAYMENT 100			19 50	357 59 LELAND E RICE CAPT FD

INSURANCE NOTICE

IMPORTANT   IF PREMIUM IS NOT PAID WHEN DUE OR WITHIN THIRTY-ONE DAYS THEREAFTER, INSURANCE WILL LAPSE. MAKE CHECKS OR MONEY ORDERS PAYABLE TO THE TREASURER OF THE U. S. AND FORWARD TO COLLECTIONS SUBDIVISION, VETERANS ADMINISTRATION, WASHINGTON 25, D. C.

48. KIND OF INSURANCE					50. EFFECTIVE DATE OF ADJUSTMENT	51. DATE OF NEXT PREMIUM DUE	52. PREMIUM DUE	53. INTENTION OF VETERAN TO
Nat. Serv.	U.S. Govt.	None	Adjusted	V. A.	MAY 46	JUNE 46	6 50	Continue Discontinue
X				X				X

55. REMARKS (This space for completion of above items or entry of other items specified in W. D. Directives)
LAPEL BUTTON ISSUED   A S R SCORE (2 SEP 45) 130

56. SIGNATURE OF PERSON BEING SEPARATED	57. PERSONNEL OFFICER (Type name, grade and organization - signature)
	G L STACKHOUSE CWO USA

Ken's honorable discharge papers - page 4.

BRAINERD, MINNESOTA

PROCLAMATION

WHEREAS, the Bataan "Death March", which took place in the Philippine Islands during World War II, was one of the cruelest acts committed against U.S. fighting men who fell into enemy hands; and

WHEREAS, the 194th Tank Battalion of Brainerd, Minnesota left Ft. Lewis, Washington in late 1941 for the Philippine Islands to help strengthen the U.S. Armed Forces, including the 31st Infantry Division, there and didn't know that they would go down into the history books of America's famous battles; and

WHEREAS, during the outbreak of World War II, the Japanese bombed Pearl Harbor and invaded the Philippine Islands to capture it and use the land mass as a "stepping stone" to conquer the Australian continent but were stopped by the U.S. Armed Forces and the Philippine Army during a five-month period until they were backed into the Bataan Peninsula where General King surrendered the American and Philippine Forces on Bataan on April 9, 1942; and

WHEREAS, these brave men, sick and wounded, lacking food, medical supplies, ammunition and armor, went into Japanese captivity and were forced to march on what is now known as the "Bataan Death March"; and

WHEREAS, of the 61 officers and enlisted men with the 194th Tank Battalion from Brainerd, only 29 survived and these men didn't know until after they were freed in 1945 (and many until long afterwards) that their battle of five months helped America and her allies to build the ships, armor, supplies, train men to fight and thus take back the lands conquered by the Emperial Japanese Forces; and

WHEREAS, all the members of that tragedy deserve to be remembered and acknowledged, especially the surviving members living in our area.

NOW, THEREFORE, I, JAMES E. WALLIN, MAYOR OF THE CITY OF BRAINERD, MINNESOTA, DO HEREBY PROCLAIM MAY 20, 2000 AS "KENNETH DAVIS DAY", AND ALONG WITH THE VETERANS OF FOREIGN WARS POST #1647, SALUTE YOU AND YOUR BRAVERY.

IN WITNESS WHEREOF, I have hereunto set my hand and caused the Seal of the City of Brainerd to be affixed this 19th day of May, 2000.

James E. Wallin
MAYOR

Brainerd, Minnesota proclaims May 20, 2000 as "Kenneth Davis Day."

11 Mr. Hospitality

When I was just twelve years old I remember my father bringing some guests home for dinner. Inviting visitors was not unusual. My father loved people. He never met a stranger, and he and my mother had the gift of hospitality. Dad was always bringing people home—for a meal, for a night, or for the entire weekend. What was unusual about these particular guests is that they were Japanese. I still remember the man's name: Tommy Tanamori. (I don't remember his wife's name.) Here was my father, who had suffered so much at the hands of the Japanese, bringing home Japanese guests for dinner and having a friendly and warm conversation with the Japanese couple. I only came to understand the full significance much later in my life.

The story is more remarkable because the young Japanese man had also suffered. Tommy Tanamori, we learned, had lost his entire family in the U.S. bombing of Hiroshima. These two men who had both suffered deeply at the hands of the armies representing the other sat in fellowship. How could this be? Because my father had learned to rise above his suffering and pain.

My father's identity was rooted in something more powerful than suffering. He was a man of deep and abiding faith. He was not primarily a WWII POW. He was not first and foremost an American soldier. My father knew that his primary identity was as a son of the living God. He was a follower of Christ, and this devotion is what defined him. Sitting with Mr. and Mrs. Tanamori, who were also followers of Jesus Christ, my dad was sitting with a brother and sister in Christ. They were family because they were part of God's family.

Mr. Tanamori had also learned to rise above his suffering and had learned something greater than suffering defined him. These two men prayed together and expressed their love for each other in spite of what they had suffered.

Their identity as brothers in Christ was greater than any pain they had endured. Their primary identity was as children of God and followers of Jesus Christ. In Christ there is no Japanese or American. In Christ there is only love that breaks down every barrier and levels every playing field. The powerful lesson against prejudice remains with me today.

This kind of visit was not an isolated event in my memories of childhood. My father had the gift of hospitality. He was always bringing someone home and they were often from a different culture or foreign country. I don't know where he found all these people, but he found them and he showed them genuine hospitality.

I remember a young man from Africa who came for a weekend. Growing up in a community that was primarily of European stock, it was not easy to find such a person. There was a university in the town where we lived, but the young man was not a university student. His dark face was not a common sight in the sleepy southern Minnesota town surrounded by farms. My father brought him home and made him part of our family life without any hesitation.

Residents of the state hospital where my father worked often were guests in our home. When Dad worked for the state hospital in St. Peter, Minnesota, he hosted a group of the residents for a regular Sunday school class. He recruited me to help him teach the class. I was only thirteen or fourteen at the time, and most kids my age were uncomfortable around people with mental and physical handicaps. At school these hospital residents who were being mainstreamed for education were the brunt of jokes and the object of derision and ridicule. My father taught me to value them. After Dad transferred to the state hospital in Brainerd, Minnesota, he brought groups of them home for a picnic and a day at the lake.

They played volleyball or croquet, and my father was the life of the party. These were people with varying degrees of mental disability, but they were treated the same as any other guest in our home. Dad's hospitality was extraordinary because it was often extended to people who could not reciprocate.

While growing up in northern Minnesota, our home always had guests during our church's summer Vacation Bible School. Our church was a very small rural church with little means. The pastor was an itinerate minister who served more than one church at a time. The members came from ten to fifteen miles around. Somehow, every summer we were blessed with visiting Vacation Bible School teachers who were missionaries to our church. We were rural urchins living fifty miles from nowhere in northern Minnesota. To a large urban church, we were seen as a mission field.

We had a small home, and it was not fancy. But my father was not concerned about the quality of our house; he was concerned about the quality of hospitality given our guests. As I look back on it now I realize that he was completely unselfconscious about our financial means. As a result, so was I. It was not until I was well into adulthood that I understood how poor we were when growing up in northern Minnesota. But every summer we gave whatever space we had, and whatever means we could, to host these young Bible school teachers from all over the country. They came to teach us about the love of Jesus. I imagine they learned something about the love of Jesus from my father too.

Whenever visitors came to our little country church, they would likely end up at the Davis house for Sunday dinner. Along with another family or two from the church, my father would gather enough people for a great game of softball or volleyball. The ritual meant we were hardly ever by ourselves as a family. Our home was always open to others and often filled with guests.

My father also learned about hospitality from strangers. I remember my father coming home one evening when he had had car trouble. He said he had stopped by the side of the road and was waiting for help. There were no cell phones at that time, so a stranded driver was totally dependent on the goodwill of passersby. A lot of very nice cars drove right past. Then an old beat-up van pulled behind my father's stalled car. Out of that van stepped a poorly dressed, long-haired, bearded hippy-type person, as my father described him. In those days, most long-haired, jean-clad young people were suspect to older adults.

At first Dad wondered about the young man's intentions, but it took little time to realize the hippy had stopped to help. My father often referred to that incident and how he learned not to judge people by what they looked like on the outside; it was an unfair stereotype.

Today, I find myself the pastor of a very diverse congregation. I am living in a community where I am an ethnic minority, and as a consequence I am learning Spanish. The congregation I serve is also generationally and financially diverse. I am ministering to and gaining much from single moms, all recovering alcoholics and drug abusers, who are being reunited with their children through a government program. From them I have learned that I am a "normie"—a normal person who has a very different life than they have had. I am excited about what I am learning from people who are very different than I am. My life is being enriched by friendships with people who have backgrounds and experiences totally foreign to me. I presently serve with a staff comprised of a Venezuelan, a Guatemalan, a Filipina, a Mexican, and a young man who is half Albanian and half Mexican. How did I get here? What was it that attracted me to this kind of a ministry? How is it that I am so comfortable in a context that is making almost everyone else very uncomfortable?

I think Dad's to blame. All my life I watched him treat everyone equally. And I watched him demonstrate that the color of a person's skin, the clothes they wear, the length of their hair, or where they are from does not matter. What matters is being kind and showing hospitality. For a man who almost died from three and a half years of inhospitality, it is remarkable he was so welcoming to others.

Perhaps because he knew so well the pain of being an unwelcome guest, he determined to make every person he encountered feel welcome. Hospitality is one of the many ways my father demonstrated his Christian faith and practiced what he understood the Bible taught. In Leviticus 19:34 the Lord reminded Israel they too were aliens (foreigners) and so ought to treat aliens among them as one of their native born—to love the stranger as yourself. My father lived this Scripture out in front of me in living color with people from all over the world.

My father was a patriot. To his dying day tears caressed his cheeks whenever he heard the national anthem played, saw a flag raised, or recited the Pledge of Allegiance. My father was a family man. He provided for and loved his wife and children. But my father's primary identity was not his nationality or his nuclear family. First and foremost he was a child of God, and that identity was more than sufficient to help him rise above what he suffered. As a result, God's love for me has always been my primary identity too. Through good times and bad, through plenty and want, the deep and abiding knowledge that I am a beloved child of God has anchored me. And the anchor provides an inner strength and perspective that allows me to be open to people who are very different. This openness I learned from my father.

12 Mr. Positive

The men who defended Bataan against the Japanese invasion are notable not because they fought. Many American soldiers fought valiantly on many fronts during WWII. The men of Bataan were notable because of the defense they were able to provide in spite of their deteriorating physical condition and with virtually no outside military support. Their defense was also unusual because so many of them were not trained as infantry. Many were sailors and airmen.[39] The Japanese plan was to take Bataan in three weeks. It took them more than four months. During that time the American and Filipino fighters were totally cut off from support and supplies, except for a few guns on Corregidor.

Unfortunately, those guns were not designed to defend Bataan. They were positioned to provide defense for Corregidor, and the "U.S. Corps of Engineers began to build fortifications on the island to secure the seaward approach to Manila Bay."[40] To make matters worse, the air support stationed on Bataan was quickly decimated by the Japanese. Despite warnings of a possible repeat performance similar to Pearl Harbor, the American air fleet was parked in full view at Clark Airfield, and the Japanese air force descended on Bataan and destroyed any possible American air support one day after Pearl Harbor.

So the defenders of Bataan had no significant artillery support and no air support. Setting up lines of defense at least three times, the American forces

---

[39]John D. Lukcas, "Triumph on 'Bataan,' " *World War II*, September-October 2010, pp. 51-57.

[40]U.S. Corps of Engineers began to build fortifications on the island to secure the seaward approach to Manila Bay. **http://www.corregidorisland.com/history.html**

were gradually cut off from all supplies on Luzon as well. By January 1942 they were on half rations. Most were already sick with malaria, dysentery, and beriberi. By March they were on quarter rations. And by the time of the surrender on April 9, 1942, the American forces were getting less than one thousand calories a day even though they were doing military maneuvers that required more than four thousand calories a day.[41] They were sick and starving when they became prisoners of war.

What was particularly notable with my dad, given all that he had suffered, was he was so positive about everything. He always had a smile on his face and lightness to his step clearly conveying optimism about life. The constant smile on his face was evident in the video review of his life at his memorial service. In every picture he was smiling (See painting page 186) or making a funny face. Because he courted death for three and a half years, he loved life. He loved a good joke and he loved to tease. As a young child I remember walking down the street in Eveleth, Minnesota, when we came to town for groceries, something we did every two or three weeks. Occasionally on these trips for necessary supplies we stopped for a hamburger at a small restaurant. Unlike today when most families dine out several meals every week, eating out was a major treat for us. After our lunch, Dad stopped at an auto supply store and purchased two tail lamp covers for one of our vehicles. Though my mother was mortified, I remember laughing hysterically as my father held those two light covers over his chest like breasts and strutted down the street.

My father loved people and he especially loved to tease girls. Any time my sister or I brought a new friend home, they would end up on his lap or on the floor with Dad threatening to give them a whisker rub. He had a five o'clock shadow two hours after shaving, so he was prepared any time. Though it was embarrassing at the time, and although today a man could get into serious trouble for this kind of behavior, my friends who were subjected to the teasing recall it with fondness. Penny Giesbrecht, a lifelong friend who was my roommate my first year in college, offered me more evidence of my father's love of life and penchant for fun. Every time Penny and I get together, she recalls coming home with me from college and how my father

---

[41]Paul Reuter, "G-4 and Surgeon of Luzon Force Report," *Battling Bastards of Bataan*, http://home.pacbell.net/fbaldie/G-4_and_Surgeon_Report.html.

greeted me. As soon as I came in the door he grabbed me and hugged me, and then got me to climb up on his back and he gave me a piggy-back ride while running around the house whooping and hollering. I am sure Penny got a little hug and a whisker rub when he was done with me. He was a fun-loving and affectionate man.

In my travels and conversations with other Bataan survivors, I have learned love of life and playfulness was not an unusual response. On my visit to Corregidor, Steve Kwiecinski, an American who leads tours of Bataan, and I spoke about how amazing it was our fathers were so positive. Steve's dad, like mine, never said a bad thing about anybody. My dad always saw possibilities and always made things work. He was definitely a "glass-half-full guy." So was Steve's father. How did this positivity happen when these men suffered so much? Four years of their lives were stolen and filled with brutality and torture. But always they had a smile and were positive. We both agreed it was a combination of their faith, the choices they made and the character they had developed. In his book "Some Survived," Manny Lawton notes "In some instances their mental and psychological strength seemed to be rooted in a deep religious faith; in others it could have been a defiance of death itself. No doubt both were factors."[42]

My dad influenced my outlook on life. Being around him made me a more positive person, one who always sees possibilities—to a fault, perhaps. I can be overly trusting and optimistic, and as a result I'm often disappointed. I remember Dad saying, "Don't believe anything you hear and only half of what you see." His warning was in relation to hearing rumors or gossip or anything that put others in a bad light. Later in life, many of my professors and many books I read taught me the same thing. When considering the words and actions of another person, assume the best of possible motives. But Dad taught it first. I am an unrepentant optimist and now understand more about why I am.

It is difficult to understand the mindset, even in a time of war, that would take these sick and starving men—about seventy thousand of them—and march them to a faraway camp (See painting page 24).

---

[42]Manny Lawton, *Some Survived* (Chapel Hill, NC: Algonquin Books, 2004), p. 46.

It's difficult enough to understand, but harder still to comprehend how the Japanese soldiers marched them, many without shoes and half dressed, with very little rest and without food and water in the relentless daytime sun, with temperatures reaching one hundred ten degrees. There was water by the roadside—rivers and artesian wells—but the prisoners were not allowed to stop. If they did, they were shot and bayoneted. The marching men saw bodies lining their path, fallen comrades whose disease and starvation could not withstand the march. If they attempted to help a fallen comrade, they were met with the butt of a gun or bayonet. They marched about fifty-five miles (See map page 101). They were allowed only a couple of brief stops, with a small amount of rice and water provided on at least one occasion at Balanga. Already sick and starving, many did not survive.

People who have studied the war and the mindset of the Japanese military have concluded at least three factors contributed to their brutality. First, was their unquestioned dedication to the emperor. The emperor was divine. So these soldiers believed they were fighting a holy war. Like contemporary Jihad, because it is a holy war, anything done in the name of the god is good. Second, the Japanese's deeply rooted sense of honor and commitment to fighting to the death meant they had a complete disdain for the American troops who had surrendered.[43] Third, the Japanese troops were furious. They had been told and were expected to conquer Bataan in three weeks. It took four months and thousands of deaths. Some believe that these three realities combined to create soldiers capable of unspeakable brutality.

After witnessing a Japanese officer beating a Japanese private who had fallen from heat and exhaustion, Bernard Fitzpatrick, a Minnesotan serving with the 194th Tank Battalion from Fort Ripley, Minnesota, explained the Japanese brutality:

> The officer immediately, as if nothing had happened, strolled to a log nearby and sat down to clean the blood from the hilt of his sword with precious care.

---

[43]"Bataan 50 Years Later," *Brainerd Daily Dispatch*, March 29, 1992, p. 1C. (The Japanese warrior code "bushido" taught that solders who surrendered were beneath contempt.)

Seeing two Americans near him he spoke casually to them in excellent English. I was one of them. Only much later did I realize that he was reacting perfectly naturally. If we had been able to comprehend his actions, this is what we would have understood. "We will treat you as we treat our own. We can in honor do no less."[44]

Given the brutality of the Death March, imagine the hope of those who still were alive after fifty-plus miles when they came to a train station and it appeared they would be taken by boxcar the rest of the way to their final destination. They must have felt such relief to think that the march was coming to an end. They must have imagined they would sit while riding the train. What horror and shock must have flooded their hearts when it became clear these box cars would provide no relief at all? Oh, yes, they would ride in box cars, but there would be no sitting or resting.

Now the same mindset that engineered the Death March engineered the death cars. Boxcars that could carry fifty men sitting were packed with up to three times that many men (See photo page 92).[45] There was no room to sit; they could only stand. If the doors had been left open, perhaps they could survive. But the doors were shut tight, leaving little ventilation for men packed like sardines, unless they were lucky enough to be standing near the cracks in the doors or near a rust hole in a wall. Bernard Fitzpatrick remembers,

> Some of the prisoners were even light-hearted at the opportunity of riding in a railroad coach after the days of agonizing walking. Our spirits dropped when the guard began forcing us with bayonets, rifle butts, and clubs into the small wooden or steel boxcars. . . . I was pushed into one . . . along with more prisoners until the car became so jammed that we were standing tight against each other.[46]

---

[44]Bernard Fitzpatrick, "Bataan," *Minneapolis Tribune*, April 19, 1981, 1E.

[45]Lawton, *Some Survived*, p. 23.

[46]Ibid.

When I visited the Capas National Monument in the spring of 2010, I touched one of these boxcars, the only one remaining of its kind. I wanted to open the door. I wanted to climb in and stand where my father stood. I cannot imagine the sounds and smells and feelings of his suffering. But touching the place, touching the thing somehow connected me more deeply to my father. Ironically, a welcome sign is sculpted in the manicured grass alongside the boxcar today. These boxcars did not welcome their prisoners. They were cages of death.

By the time they were removed from the boxcars, the men—all with dysentery—were standing in human excrement. The men who were suffocating had scratched and clawed and flailed to stay alive, leaving those around them further injured and bleeding. The box-cars were no relief from the Death March. The box-car ride was a death ride. When the railroad cars finally came to a stop forty miles later and the doors were opened, many men fell out dead. Yet even the end of the ride was not the end of their agony. Now the Japanese marched them another six miles to Camp O'Donnell (See photo page 92).[47]

---

[47]Ibid., pp. 78-79. "Maurice de Saxe, marshal general of France, believed that 'the severest discipline' produced 'the greatest deeds,' and across the ages, East and West men pressed into service often learned the lesson of discipline under duress. The Germans favored the whip, the French the fist. In the Imperial Japanese Army, The 'encouragement' (*bentatsu* it was called) turned the training camps of Hokkaido, Honshu, Shikoku, and Kyushu into alembics, a closed world of violence where men were subjected to the most brutal system of army discipline in the world. Here the civilian in a man, all he had been or wanted to be, was beaten out of him. What was left were hollow men, automatons living in a space, as one recruit put it, where 'all the breathable air seemed to be exhausted,' a 'zone of emptiness.' One group of primitives had created from itself another group of primitives, and all the groups from all the camps across all the home islands formed one great primal horde, 2,287,000 men who had been savaged to produce an army of savage intent."

By the time they reached the camp, estimates of casualties range from twelve to twenty thousand. In the next six weeks at O'Donnell many more would perish. The men faced hell on earth, with no end in sight.[48]

Visiting the monument to O'Donnell and those who lost their lives there was a sacred experience. As I ran my fingers over the letters of the names of the men who died, I felt connected to them in some strange way. I knelt down and touched the letters of the name "Camp O'Donnell" and somehow felt like I was touching my dad.

I walked over to the barbed-wire fence along the edge of the monument property. On the other side of the fence, stood several white steers. Ribs protruding, they looked undernourished (See painting page 82). They stared back at me. I could not help but think how strange this was. Here was a barbed-wire fence keeping what looked to be starving animals out where once such fences kept starving men in. And yet how tragic because these skinny cattle certainly were better kept than the men imprisoned here more than sixty years ago.

I also visited Mariveles, at the southern end of the Bataan Peninsula where the Death March began. There stands the first of one hundred twelve kilometer markers that line the Bataan Death March route. On a bright, sunny Tuesday morning, my husband and I along with Steve and Marcia Kwiecinski walked the first sixteen kilometers of the Death March route. It was March and the temperature was above ninety degrees. I stopped as often as I liked to get water from stands along the way. I had a full stomach and had been eating beyond my needed calories for many days. I had an umbrella to shade me and good walking shoes on my feet. It still was a difficult walk.

---

[48]"Approximately 1,600 Americans died in the first forty days in Camp O'Donnell. Almost 20,000 Filipinos died in their first four months of captivity, in the same camp. It did not have the sanitation sub-structure or water supply necessary to hold such a large amount of men. Many died from diseases they had since Bataan. Many caught new diseases while at the camp. There was little medicine available to the prisoners. Their inadequate diets also contributed to the high death rate. And the Japanese soldiers continued to murder and mistreat their captives. Due to the high death rate in Camp O'Donnell the Japanese transferred all Americans to Cabanatuan north of Camp O'Donnell on June 6, 1942, leaving behind five hundred as caretakers and for burial detail. They in turn were sent to Cabanatuan on July 5, 1942. The Filipino prisoners were paroled beginning in July 1942" ("Outline of Events," *Battling Bastards of Bataan*, April 4, 1998, http://home.pacbell.net/fbaldie/Outline.html).

I could not imagine the conditions my father walked in. It must have seemed like hell on earth. For me, it was such a privilege to walk even a small part of the route and see the same terrain my father saw.

As I looked around I saw the mountain range off in the distance. Dad too saw these mountains. Along the road I could see artesian wells. My father talked about these and what hazards they became as thirsty, starving men broke lines to try to get a drink. I could still see nipa huts made of grass and bamboo like my father had told me about in his stories describing the countryside. As we passed fields of rice and sugarcane, stories my father told me flooded my mind, and my eyes filled with tears. We passed several domestic cattle that stopped their grazing to see these strange foreigners walking along their pastures. (I could not help but think of a Gary Larson *Far Side* cartoon and its possible caption.) My father told me stories of stealing, killing, and eating these domesticated cattle in order to stay alive during the battle for Bataan.

I was walking the path freely of my own choosing. My father walked it at the end of a bayonet with men falling and dying all along the way. He walked it not for sixteen kilometers but for seventy or eighty kilometers day and night for three to five days without rest or sleep. He had an empty stomach and no water. He could not stop and rest, and had no shade. He was malnourished and sick with malaria and beriberi and severe diarrhea. The road, the very road my feet were on, was the same route my father walked. Asphalt now covers what was mainly a dirt and concrete highway then, but this was the path he took. And I was on it.

It is impossible to describe all the things I felt as I looked down the long road and imagined seeing men marching on a dirt road three to five abreast as far as the eye could see. I imagined the dead bodies strewn along the way. I imagined the sound of so much suffering. And I heard the question people have asked me over and over again: "How did he survive?" How did any of them survive? It took uncommon will, uncommon strength, and no small amount of the sheer grace and providence of God. So many perished. How grateful I am my father did survive. How much more respect and admiration I have for him now because I understand more about what he endured.

The pain and suffering of these men is hard to imagine. Yet many did survive the horror of these experiences. And many did more than survive. Many rose above their suffering and pain to become powerful examples of what it means to overcome adversity and to turn tragedy into opportunity. Living with death as a constant companion made them love life. Living under such negative circumstances for so long made them positive about everything, once they survived. My father was one of those men.

I don't remember my father being negative about anything. He was gruff at times, but in some ways sternness was characteristic of his generation's take on parenting. Richard Rohr describes the approach succinctly:

> The Father symbolizes that part of God that demands and desires his sons and daughters to become all they can be, that demanding expectant part of God. Parents surely see that in relationship to their children. Why it is sometimes hard to be soft or nice to them. If I don't teach them this, you say, then they will screw up or not live a good life; I've got to help them in this way. I've got to teach them. We call this the angry God in the Old Testament. That's not the right word. It's the expectant part of love, the part of love that pushes a bit. It's tough love. It's a necessary part of love.[49]

Dad was demanding, but never negative. At least that was my experience of him. We grew up in churches that often experienced conflict. My father, being a natural leader, was always heavily involved in the affairs of the church. Through all those years and all those conflicts, people from the church would call our home to talk to my father. Now that I have been a pastor and church leader for many years, I understand all too well the dynamics of organizational conflict. In all the times of conflict I do not ever remember hearing my father speak ill of another person, let alone demonize them, as often happens in conflicts involving deeply held values and convictions. He would always talk about the people involved in the conflict in a way that gave them the benefit of the doubt. He did not attribute motives. He did not take sides. As I recall, he always sought to be the mediator and the reconciler.

---

[49]Richard Rohr, *Radical Grace* (Cincinnati: St. Anthony Messenger Press, 1995), pp. 203-5.

I remember hearing him correct someone when he knew the information was false or incomplete, and I remember him encouraging people to speak and act in ways that were in keeping with biblical teaching. But I do not remember him going off on a tirade about this or that person, as I have often experienced in the midst of church conflicts. People called my father because they knew he was a positive person and was primarily a reconciler and a peacemaker. If they called just to get support for "their side," he quickly put that notion to rest. He seemed to be able to recognize the good intentions behind even bad behavior. He could have used all the attention for his own personal ego and power, but he didn't. He was dedicated to making the church more of what Christ called it to be, and he modeled his positive outlook on the future of the church even when it was embroiled in conflict.

I am often embarrassed at my own naiveté and gullibility. I am often teased for these things. I realize that both my personal and professional life have been dramatically shaped by the man who survived three and a half years as a prisoner of war. I spent a lot of time with him growing up. I didn't spend time in the kitchen learning to cook or in the house learning to knit or make beautiful things. I was in the garage and on the rooftop. I know the tool box and how to drive a nail. I was under the hood of the car and know the parts of an engine. I am a fixer because I was with my dad when he was fixing all sorts of things. More than the mechanical ability I gained from being with him, I gained an attitude. I inherited the belief that if I put my mind to it, I could do anything. I learned the habit of believing everything was possible and everything was redeemable.

Very little was thrown away in my father's garage. It was all useful. Anything could be fixed. His attitude has shaped my professional life, and as I work with people I find myself equally optimistic. Everyone has value and can contribute to community. Everyone, with God's help, is fixable. There are no throwaways in God's spiritual economy. Of course, as age has seasoned my experience I realize that there are people and circumstances so complex and so deeply broken they will never be completely fixed in this life. But this life is only a path to the next, where all things will be made new! Understanding this means we can get started now. Even when we don't see the end result now, we will in the next life. This belief fuels my inherited optimism even more.

My dad was forged by war. I was too, as were all the members of my family. My children have been forged by it as well. And much of what America was able to accomplish and become, I believe, is due to the character of these men who survived WWII and served their families and their country as well after the war as they did during it. My dad was a positive man. He appreciated every day of life, every plate of food, and every friend and acquaintance. He was amazing. He shaped my outlook on life. I am grateful to have been raised by Mr Positive.

O'DONNELL BURIAL DUTY
Oil Painting, 2010

13 The Hell Ship *Noto Maru*

The same brutality that engineered the Bataan Death March (and the death cars) would rear its ugly head again beginning in the summer of 1944, when the Japanese began loading Allied troops from the POW camps onto Japanese cargo ships. They packed the POWs like sardines into the hold of the ships (See photo and painting page 95). A latrine was provided in the middle of the hold, but in order to get to it men had to crawl over each other. My father said the effort resulted in more difficulty and pain than the "relief" was worth. Most could not make it to the latrine in time, anyway. As a result, again, the men, all with dysentery, found themselves sitting and standing in human excrement. Because the journey lasted from two weeks to as long as two months the excrement was much deeper than in the box cars.

In a newspaper interview published in the *Brainerd Daily Dispatch* on April 7, 1967, Dad described what he remembered about the *Noto Maru*.

> The only way there was enough room was for the men to sit between each other's knees. There was a big bucket in the middle of the room for wastes. If you didn't make it in time, it was just tough. There was a guard at the opening of the hold with a machine gun.

Against the rules of the Geneva Convention, these Japanese ships were unmarked. As a result, they were often torpedoed by American submarines. Many were damaged.

Some were sunk and thousands of American POWs perished in the holds of these ships[50] sunk by American torpedoes.[51] Of the convoy of ships that left the harbor around the same time as the *Noto Maru*, it was the last ship to leave that was not damaged or sunk by an American torpedo. My father did not tell me about this brush with death.

The *Noto Maru* was fired upon but the torpedo missed. There were those who wished the torpedo would have hit. A POW explained in an interview with Adrian Martin:

> Pretty soon we could hear this thunder, and what it was. They were rollin' depth charges off the aft end of the ship because of our submarines. Believe it or not, I hoped to hell we got hit. Kill us all. Blow us sky high. Then pretty soon it calmed down. [52]

Those men in the ships that survived the voyage did not fare much better. Once in a while their captors would send down cups of dry, uncooked rice and a few cups of water. The grossly inadequate ration benefited few. And, when the ships pulled into the harbors of their destination many were taken out dead.

My father's ship had one thousand thirty-five prisoners of war on board. Their journey was relatively short compared to other POW cargo transports, and consequently none of the prisoners perished during the transport.

---

[50]Michael Norman and Elizabeth M. Norman, *Tears in the Darkness* (New York: Farrar, Straus, Giroux, 2009), pp. 305-6. "Between January 1942 and July 1945, the Japanese transported 156 shiploads of Allied POWs from battlefields and camps in the southwest Pacific to slave labor sites in their territories and home islands. Although they packed the prisoners in the same spaces they used for their own trips, they stuffed those spaces as if they were shipping livestock, then, out of expediency, spite, or both, denied them adequate air, food, and water. More than 126,000 Allied prisoners of war and native laborers made these journeys, and more than 21,000 died en route or went down with the ships."

[51]"Outline of Events," *Battling Bastards of Bataan*
<http://home.pacbell.net/fbaldie/Outline.html>.

[52]Adrian Martin, *Brothers from Bataan* (Manhattan, Kan.: Sunflower University Press, 1992), pp. 192-93.

Of course, many continued to die in the days and weeks that followed. But of the five hundred thirty five that went to Hanawa, Sendai No. 6, in northern Japan, only eight died before liberation in September of 1945. One of them was Adrian R. Martin. His nephew by the same name researched extensively and wrote about Hanawa. In his book, *Brothers from Bataan: POWs 1942-1945*, he writes:

> Death was nothing new to the Battling Bastards of Bataan. Once the fighting started in 1941 in the Philippines, the word was on their lips and in their minds daily. After they surrendered in 1942 and the fighting stopped, death didn't go away. It followed them along the Death March to Camp O'Donnell, then to Cabanatuan ...and continued with them on the hell ships bound for Japan. Somewhat ironic about the Hanawa men is that after three years as prisoners and in a weakened condition, only eight died during the twelve months that Hanawa was in operation. Credit certainly has to go to Dr. Jackson, Dr. Lamy, and Dr. Golenternek.[53]

Another survivor, named Cole, gave further reason why no one died on the *Noto Maru*. In Adrian Martin's interview, he says, "The Japs kept the hatch covers open, and by the way, that's important because on many of the hell ships where the guys died, they kept the hatch closed. So we got some air." [54]

My father told me about the hell ships, but only mentioned them briefly. He did not go into much detail. I did not fully realize the appropriateness of their name until I studied further and talked to other men who survived them. These ships were living hell. Many of the men went crazy. Others found ingenious ways to make the hell more bearable. Again, Martin's interviews are revealing.

> Once they saw that the hold could hold all of us, they ordered us to sit down. We could only sit in each other's laps. This is when the heat

---

[53]Ibid., pp. 250-51.

[54]Ibid., p. 192.

exhaustion struck us. I was one of those that passed out. After I came to, I took the blanket I was carrying and strung it between the I-beans on the overhead of the hold. That helped ease the overcrowding. Others who had blankets and a rope did the same.[55]

True to form, most of these brave men did not talk about their ordeal until much later in life. Then they spoke of it only when hounded and prodded by inquiring historians and relatives interested in keeping alive the memory of what happened for their children and grandchildren. Today, technological media can put world events as they occur in people's living rooms and on their computer screens. It was not always so. Only recently did I learn that the government and people of the United States did not know about the Death March until 1944, when an American prisoner escaped and made his way back to the States and told the story of the treatment of the Bataan soldiers. His story greatly heightened the urgency of the United States' return to the Pacific and resulted in more concentrated efforts to liberate them. Unfortunately, the Japanese also acted with urgency and they began shipping the Bataan prisoners en masse all over the Pacific Rim.

During my visit to the Philippine Islands I was able to visit two places that are significant to the stories of the hell ships. Subic Bay has a memorial to those who perished and survived these boats from hell. The beautiful black marble monument is such a contrast to the words etched on them describing the horrific conditions of the ships. The monument stands with the backdrop of the bay where many of these ships had been anchored. The beautiful blue serene waters of the bay were a stark contrast to the horrors of the ships that left the place. Even though my father's ship did not embark from Subic Bay, I again felt connected by him to all those who like him endured so much suffering on these ships.

Later I visited the pier in Manila harbor where more of the hell ships sailed for Japan, including the *Noto Maru*. I stood on the pier looking out over the water thinking, *this is where my father*

---

[55]Joe Zorzanello, quoted in ibid., p. 191.

waited for more than a day in the hold of a ship before it embarked. In these waters his ship, packed with sick and dying men who had been prisoners for more than two years, waited to be taken to another place of imprisonment, another year of unknown horrors. In this place my father, somehow with a light in his eyes and his jaw set hard, determined to survive.

These men, who survived unspeakable horrors, did not talk of them when they came home. My aunt Ruthie went to see my father when he returned to Seattle in October 1945. She and others like her were briefed by officials before they saw their loved ones. It was explained that the men were improving in health but still not well. They had been fed well and had gained weight but would have difficulties related to digestion and elimination. They also were told *not* to ask them questions about their time as prisoners. I wonder what the motivation was for the advice. Certainly it was an era that was not as self-reflective and psychologically inquisitive, but I believe it was a form of governmental self-protection. Given the scope and scale of WWII and all of the prisoners returning, the government was not prepared to handle the post-traumatic effects of the war. There was no post-traumatic stress disorder diagnosis, and they likely believed that the best way for the government to ensure success in re-acclimation of all of those returning was to leave well enough alone.

Actually, my father told me about one appointment he had with a psychiatrist. Dad was quite clear that the session was not at all helpful. He remembers it being very odd and wondered if the doctor himself had mental problems! The psychiatrist asked him questions like, "Do you ever think about having sex with your mother?" and "Do you fantasize about killing a woman after you have sex with her?" Dad said he was totally turned off by the doctor's questions and as a result did not want to talk to him about anything. Being that those years were dominated by Freudian psychology, which views almost all of human behavior through the lens of sexual repression, the kind of questioning Dad endured is not all that surprising. Needless to say, the psychotherapy did not provide much relief.

I can't help but believe that the "don't ask" instruction was in hopes that the memories would go away and the soldiers would proceed to adjust happily to life as free men. No one knows fully the consequence of this negligence. But in addition to the generation's sense of duty and lack of self-concern, it resulted in many of us not hearing the stories that so shaped us, our families and our country.[56]

My father was a God-fearing man. He was a hell-fearing man. He believed in both because he had experienced both. He had experienced the power of God that sustained him throughout his three and a half years as a prisoner of war. And he had experienced hell, or at least the closest thing to it on earth. Thank God that by His grace and power my father, in spite of the *Noto Maru*, had a tomorrow! In spite of all he suffered and all the times he brushed the face of death, he survived. And he became a man who was positively determined to make the most of every day of life he was given.

---

[56]"After they were released these men they were sent to various military hospitals for physical examinations. Many of their ailments due to malnutrition went undiagnosed. Many of the systemic fevers they had contracted went undiagnosed. More importantly, the psychological scars they suffered were never recognized. It was not until years after the Vietnam War the US government recognized "post-traumatic stress disorder" or PTSD, as a legitimate disorder. It is safe to say each of these men has carried these scars for the rest of their lives and indirectly so did their families" ("Outline of Events," *Batting Bastards of Bataan*, April 1998 < http://home.pacbell.net/fbaldie/Outline.html>).

MINE SMOKE STACK
Pencil Drawing, 2010

14 Laboring in a Copper Mine

I used to dream about it often, but I never thought I would actually be able to visit the places my father spent as a prisoner of war. I thank God for the Lily Foundation and their support of pastor sabbaticals. When my application for one of the grants was approved I could hardly believe it was true. I was going to the Philippine Islands and Japan! In addition to Paul Fukuda, a good friend named Masako Kim, who I met when I was serving as a director of children's ministries in Wichita, Kansas, in the late 1980s, was an invaluable help to me in preparing for the journey. Masako is Japanese and travels to Japan often. She also put me in contact with another Japanese couple who lived near me in southern California. Mr. and Mrs. Yamada graciously received me into their home and helped to orient me for my travel to Japan.

So in March 2010 my husband and I went to Japan to see the place my father labored as a prisoner of the Japanese. In the summer of 1944 as the tide of the war was clearly turning against the Japanese they began shipping prisoners en masse all over the Pacific Rim to work in factories that produced "war essentials." My father was shipped on the *Noto Maru* to Japan and was then transported by train to northern Japan. The camp was called Hanawa or Sendai No. 6. It was the Osarizawa mine near Kazuno City in Akita Prefecture.

It was a long but beautiful train ride from Tokyo. The Japanese countryside is lush. The small villages that line the railway are neat and clean and surrounded by productive agriculture of all kinds.[57] The train had stewards who walked the cars with carts filled with food and drink of all kinds.

---

[57] The train route went right through the city of Sendai and very near the nuclear power plant that was seriously damaged by the earthquake and subsequent tsunami of March 2011. It is tragic to think that many of these idyllic villages full of life are now destroyed and lifeless.

As we traveled north, the greenery began to subside and patches of snow began to appear. The fresh snow and dark leafless trees covered the mountain ranges making them look like velvet paintings. (See photo page 96). Though we were not prepared adequately for it, Kazuno City, where Hanawa, Sendai No. 6, was located, was in the midst of winter.

My father never told me about the train to Hanawa (See map page 102). And although we were on a modern bullet train, I later learned we rode the same rail route my father took to Hanawa in September 1944. I since have read about this part of my father's experience in Adrian Martin's book *Brothers from Bataan: POWs 1942-1945*.

> Although they [the POWs he interviewed] disagree as to what method they journeyed from Moji, they are unanimous in affirming that the train ride north and the food served were the best part of their travel to their Japanese camp.

A POW named Nix described it this way.

"The train did not have enough room for everybody. Sometimes to get rest you had to get down underneath the seats on the floor… or kind of just lay in the aisles."

Another POW, Throneberry, said, "I remember getting a box lunch aboard the train… [I]t contained a little rice, maybe some squid, and some seaweed. It was the best meal I had in Japan."

A diary by a POW named Norquist recorded,

"Got off the train at about 3:00 a.m. and were marched to some sheds where we were allowed to wash up and rest awhile. We each got a box of rice and another box containing a pickle, a salted plum, a bit of fish, a piece of cucumber and a little dried seaweed. To that hungry mob, this breakfast was a feast."[58]

---

[58]All quotes of POWs from Adrian Martin, *Brothers from Bataan* (Manhattan, Kan: Sunflower University Press, 1992), pp. 196-99.

The relative comfort was short-lived for the men sent to Hanawa, Sendai No. 6. Once they arrived at Hanawa, their circumstances quickly matched and rivaled the deprivation they had known in the Philippine Islands' POW camps. After being a prisoner in the brutally hot and humid climate of the Philippine Islands, the new environment was brutally cold. Although the barracks were new and built in a much colder climate, they were very similar in design to the ones the POWs had left in the Philippines. They were made of wood and had no heat.[59] There were forty-five to fifty men in each barrack and they slept on two-level bamboo bunks with only a straw mat for padding. Their clothes were not designed for the climate either. According to my father, their pants and jackets were made of burlap and their shoes were made of straw. As a result the POWs had a lot of trouble with their feet.

In this uniform the men walked daily up a steep incline a couple of miles, three or four kilometers, to the mine, and back down again at the end of the day. My father remembered five to six inches of snow being on the ground. When we were there in March 2010, there was almost three feet of snow still on the ground. It was cold and windy even though we were dressed better than the POWs were. The scenery, once again, was breathtaking. The surrounding snow-capped mountains covered with trees against the pale blue sky were peaceful. It was difficult to fathom that this view was what my father saw each day he walked to and from the mines. As was the case when I walked the route of the Bataan Death March, I felt a deep sadness at the disparity between what I was seeing and what I knew my father experienced here.

My father began working deep in the mines (See photos page 96). He thought it was about eight hundred feet that he walked up and down daily in the mine. For a healthy, well-fed man the hike would be a formidable workout. But for a sick and malnourished man it would seem impossible.

---

[59]Ibid. Diagrams by Capt. E. Pearce Fleming, one of the officers in Hanawa, show three "small stoves" in each barrack; a description taken from documents available through the American Ex-Prisoners of War Association says that the barracks were "very inadequately heated" (p. 210).

By this time in his imprisonment he probably weighed barely more than one hundred pounds. Estimates from medical experts based on their POW diet and the work they were being forced to do meant they lost on average twenty-five pounds a year. This estimate matches my father's experience. In three and a half years he lost about seventy-five to eighty-five pounds.

After a while, Dad did not remember how long, he was assigned to the top of the mine, where he dumped the ore carts and recorded the amount being extracted. (It was here that he encountered the guard he called a "good man.")

When I was in Kazuno-Hanawa I was able to visit the Osarizawa mine.[60] It is no longer an operating mine but a tourist site and an educational center. Tours are conducted for visitors and school children to see the wonders of a mine that goes miles into the earth and has hundreds of miles of tunnels. When we were there, the mine tours were not open yet due to the winter climate of the region, but we were given a special private tour arranged by one of the city employees. His name was Mr. Sato. Nori Nagasawa,[61] a member of the Japanese-American ex-POW dialogue group dedicated to fostering reconciliation between Japanese and Americans, had arranged for Mr. Sato to assist us.

One of the first things I encountered visiting the mine was the unexpected sound of children singing coming from the mine tunnels. The mine had been wired for sound, and recordings of children singing echoed through the mine. I was already feeling a heavy sadness as we began to enter the mine. Being in the very place where my father had labored as a prisoner, sick and starving, was difficult enough.

---

[60]The Japanese captured nearly 350,000 prisoners in their early conquests. Many were native prisoners who were released when they agreed not to resist the Japanese. But they kept about 140,000 Western prisoners of which 36,000 were held in camps in Japan. Another 11,000 prisoners perished when the unmarked Japanese cargo ships (hell ships) used for transport to Japan were torpedoed by Allied submarines. An additional 3,500 died while imprisoned. At the outset about 130 camps existed in Japan. Some were closed and by war's end only about 90 remained. www.powresearch.jp/en/archive/camplist/index.html.

[61] See photo page 113.

I felt like I was floating above the ground and the tour guide's voice was hollow and small, as if it was coming from a distance even though he was standing right in front of me. The sound of singing children ran counter to my sadness and anger for what I knew happened in this place. It felt so contrived and so artificial. Part of me wanted to turn around and run out of the mine. But part of me wanted to continue because I wanted to go deeper into the mine to be where my father had been. I took a deep breath and determined to compartmentalize what I was hearing and feeling. I would listen to the tour guide to some degree, but I would also just soak in the mine's smells and textures and natural sounds.

The tour exhibited mine equipment and operations that dated from after WWII. Though the tour guide acknowledged that prisoners worked the mines during the war he was either lying or totally unaware of the conditions under which the prisoners labored. Throughout the tour he proudly described all of the effort to keep the workers safe and healthy. The site signage did the same. It displayed fairly modern mine machinery and manikins in full uniforms with gas masks and safety helmets. The model workers had electric power drills and small front-end loaders. I asked the tour guide, "Are you telling me all of this equipment and these safety features were here during the war?" Without hesitation he answered, "Yes." Later in the tour I was able to see an old photograph of mine workers and I took a picture of it. Though the workers pictured appeared to be Asian, Koreans most likely, the crude equipment and the poor clothing and lack of any safety equipment more accurately reflected my father's description of working in the mine.

I had to fight back the impulse to respond with anger and incredulity! But the guide had promised me samples of ore taken from the mine when we completed the tour, and I wanted a piece of the earth to take home with me. I wanted to have a part of the place where my father almost died.

I kept my mouth shut. I chose, as my father had taught me, to assume the best of possible motives. I chose to believe that the man was just ignorant of the history and simply trained to teach school children and tourists about the glory of the mine at its height of production after the war.

The choice was somewhat vindicated later in the day when the man who arranged the tour took us to the site of the Hanawa Camp. A beautiful new middle school is now gracing the property. The city manager told us that most of the people living in the neighborhood, including the children who attend the school, do not know they live at the location of a prisoner of war camp where men who were sick and malnourished were forced to work long hours in a cold and unsafe mine doing hard labor. They, like many Japanese, are ignorant of the darker side of the history of the POWs in Japan during WWII.

Our guide parked our van in the school parking lot. I told everyone else they could stay in the car. I did not need an interpreter and I really wanted to walk in the place alone. I just needed, once again, to put my feet on the ground where my dad had been. I wanted to look around and take in the view—to see what he saw. Though certainly the view had changed some over the years, the mountains were the same. The crisp winter air was the same. I could see part of the mine complex off in the distance (See drawings pages 133 and 141). I walked along the sidewalk near the front of the new school building and imagined the barracks that once lined the property. The contrast between what I was seeing and what my father had told me was hard to hold together.

The beautiful school, educating children, stood where my father and approximately five hundred other men were brutalized for over a year. A beautiful color banner announcing the upcoming graduation draped across the railing along the sidewalk. I imagined what the school grounds must sound like when the yard and rooms are filled with the voices of children laughing and playing in the rooms and in the yard of the school. In contrast I imagined the nightmarish screams of the men who labored in the mines all day and struggled to sleep at night.

Racked with pain, infested with lice, and starving, sleep was fitful when it came. The tears came again. I could not help but wonder what these children were learning. Will their history books ever tell them about what happened on the property many decades ago? Will their teachers ever tell them about WWII and the suffering that it caused? I hope so. I know that some Japanese citizens, like Mr. Sato and Nori Nagasawa, are working hard to this end and teaching others about these lessons of history.

MINE BUILDINGS
Pencil Drawing, 2010

15   A New World

Before my trip to Japan I had the privilege of meeting and visiting with an older Japanese couple who live near me in the suburbs of Los Angeles. Mr. and Mrs. Yamada, as I mentioned earlier, were very helpful in my preparation for visiting Japan. They were both in high school in Japan during the war and attended a Christian university in Japan after the war was over. They too corroborated the story of ignorance of most of the Japanese people regarding the existence of POW camps and the brutal treatment of prisoners. They said that they did not learn about the presence of POW camps in Japan until they immigrated to the United States.

Then there are those Japanese citizens who at some point have come to know the truth and are working to bridge the cultural divide. Some of them experienced pain as Japanese civilians caught in the war, particularly during the American air raid on Tokyo. I had the privilege of meeting and getting to know one such woman. Her name is Nori Nagasawa (See photo page 97). She is in her eighties and is one of the founding members of a group called POW Research Network Japan. For almost twenty years she has sought out American ex-POWs of Japan and devoted time to developing relationships that might bring reconciliation. She works tirelessly helping the organization in any way that she can.

Her desire to do this work was birthed out of her own painful experience. She heard an American ex-POW talking disparagingly about the Japanese and she became angry and wanted to lash out at the man. She wanted to tell him about the pain and agony she experienced as a young teenager in Tokyo during the American air raids. As she listened to the man, she heard his story and realized he had a very similar story to hers.

He was using some of the same language to describe how he felt and how it had shaped his life. After some initial harsh words between them, Nori and the man decided to continue their conversation in order to learn more about the other and perhaps experience some healing through it. The idea caught on as others joined them in the dialogue and relationships which rose above their individual painful experiences developed. For the last thirty years they have met every year in Hawaii to continue the dialogue. They now work to bring others together in the dialogue in hopes of creating a new world.

I was introduced to Nori through Roger Mansell, director of the Center for Research, Allied POWS under the Japanese. He recommended Nori to help guide my husband and me on our trip to Japan to visit the mine in Akita Prefecture in northern Japan. She was incredible. The man she wanted to guide us was an older gentleman who did not want to drive to the mine when there was still snow on the ground. So he arranged another guide for us from the Hanawa city hall. His name was Mr. Tazawa, but we came to know him as Shuhei. He was a nice young man, just out of college, who spoke enough English to be helpful. He picked us up at the train station and took us to lunch. After picking up another city employee, Mr. Sato, who arranged our tour of the mine, we picked up another person to translate for us. She was a young woman teaching English at a local school. How surprised we were when she jumped in the car with us and said, "Hi guys! My name is Charlotte and I am from Santa Monica!" We were given the royal treatment from these city employees, and I know part of that was a result of Nori's association with the Japanese ex-POW dialogue group and all the work she did on our behalf.

Nori went above and beyond the call of duty. She found a hotel for us in Tokyo and visited it to make sure it was adequate. She met us at the train station to make sure we found our way safely to our hotel. She sent me detailed instructions about how and when and where to take the train when we headed north to the mine. When we returned to Tokyo she called to find out how our trip went and to make sure we got the help we needed from our guides.

Through all these arrangements, she expressed her desire to help reconciliation happen between Japanese and American people. It worked. I have a new friend in Tokyo, and I have a better understanding of the suffering that many Japanese civilians endured as a result of the war. Additionally, she is more active than many people half her age, which also inspired me.

Mr. Sato, the city employee who organized our tour and went with us to the mine, also went out of his way to express a desire for reconciliation. Though the mine tour guide was ignorant of the wartime history of the mine and the camp associated with it, Mr. Sato was not. He took special effort to point out to us information in the mine museum that acknowledged that POWs had worked there and perished in the work. He also took us to a cemetery we did not know about and showed us the gravestone that acknowledged the foreign workers who had died in the mine (See photo page 97). He guided us without a coat, boots or gloves, in the bitter wind and three feet of snow. He stomped a path through the unshoveled snow so we could walk more easily behind him in order to see the memorial to the American POWs who died. I know he is a good man. And I know it is a new world

16 The Not-so Closet Evangelist

To really understand who my father was, you need to know what he believed. My father was very bold and generous in sharing his faith. Neighbors, family members, and complete strangers were all certain to hear in some fashion about how much God loved them and that Christ died for them. It was a well-known fact in the Davis household that if any of us brought a friend home, two things would happen. They would go fishing with Dad, either on the boat when the water was open or in the fish house when the lake was frozen, and they would hear the gospel. Captive in the boat or the fish house, there was nowhere to run or hide. Dad would find a way to turn whatever conversation ensued into an opportunity to share the good news of Jesus with them. He was not timid about his faith. The evangelist was definitely out of the closet.

I remember Dad telling me how he often was ridiculed at his workplace for being outspoken about his faith. He said occasionally when he would walk down the halls of the state hospital where he worked, some of the other employees as they passed him in the halls would stretch their arms out and hang their head, mimicking Christ on the cross. They thought the gesture was an insult. For my father it was a threefold badge of honor. First, that they knew he was a Christian. Second, that they knew the message that Christ had died on a cross. And, third, that he was known for sharing the message. There is one more story I need to tell about the not-so-closeted evangelist. It's not about his war experiences, but it so embodies who my father was.

I worked with Alzheimer patients for three years as a volunteer. I am grateful because the experience helped prepare me for my own family's tragic confrontation of the disease when in 1999 we learned Dad had Alzheimer's.

One of the main things I learned working with these dear people is how certain memories remain even when all others are lost. People stricken with Alzheimer's disease often retain long-term memories even though their short-term memory is completely gone. But the retained memory is very selective.

One area of memory that has been documented to be quite often retained among Alzheimer's patients has to do with religious symbolism and meaning. In the nursing home where I volunteered, the residents did not know their own names or where they grew up, but many could recite the Lord's Prayer or the Twenty-third Psalm word for word.

I experienced this selective memory with my father in a time that was both tender and humorous. He and my mother were visiting us in Chicago. (This was the same visit when he helped me finish my antique trunk.) We decided to take him to see the Billy Graham Center for Evangelism on the campus of Wheaton College in Wheaton, Illinois. The center has a beautiful tribute to Billy Graham in the form of a very moving multisensory display of the gospel message. I knew my father would love to see it. The exhibit took us through a small, dark hall shaped like a cross, symbolizing the death of Christ. Then it suddenly opened into a light-filled room painted with sky and clouds and the rays of the sun breaking through. The words of John 3:16 are boldly written across the sky. "For God so loved the world that he gave his only begotten Son that whosoever believes in him, shall not perish, but have everlasting life." The death of Christ on the cross leads to life eternal for all of us. These truths have been and remain Billy Graham's gospel message. My father's also shared the same message to anyone who would listen.

When we came to the final room with the promise of eternal life, my father simply stood, looked around and kept saying how wonderful it was—not just the room but the gospel message. Everyone needed to know the message. After all, God so loved the world—that's everybody!

As we were leaving the Billy Graham Center, we were about half way down the steps of the building when we realized Dad was not with us. A couple of us went back to find him. As we approached the door to the center, Dad was just coming out smiling like crazy. It was obvious he was beyond pleased. Without us asking, he commenced to tell us that he had just witnessed to the women at the reception desk. He had shared the gospel with the front desk receptionists at the Billy Graham Center for Evangelism! The Alzheimer's disease had not yet robbed him of his ability to share the greatest message on earth. His deeply-rooted faith in Christ and his understanding of the need to share it with others remained intact even though perhaps his judgment about when and where to do it was compromised. Oh, if only the rest of us were so zealous to share the good news of God's love demonstrated in Christ and would come out of the closet to share our faith!

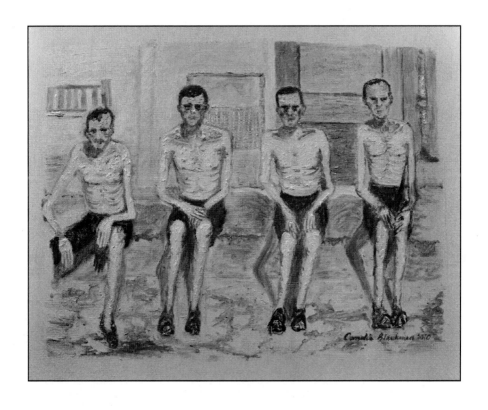

SURVIVORS
Oil Painting, 2010

17 Not Mr Perfect

I don't want to leave the impression that my father was perfect. Being a minister I have sat through many eulogies at funerals that seem to suggest the deceased was perfect—not a single flaw to recall. It is common for people to selectively remember their deceased loved ones as larger than life. It is part of the grieving process. But honesty demands we eventually come to grips with the human frailty of our lost loved ones. In honor of my father I have interviewed, researched, traveled, and reflected on his story as a means of understanding myself better. But also I have done this to pass on to my children a story that needs to be remembered. It is an extraordinary story, and my father was an extraordinary person, but he was not perfect.

Dad could be very gruff at times. The brusque nature too was part of the military imprint on his life. As loving, kind, and tender-hearted as he was, for some reason when we were growing up almost all instructions were barked military style. There was little conversation and seldom any discussion. These were orders, and you followed them. If there was any resistance or attempt to negotiate, his tone could become very harsh. He never hollered. I don't remember him raising his voice, but the tone of his voice and the set of his jaw clearly communicated there was no changing his mind; we were simply to do as he said.

I often wanted to just talk to my dad. I wanted to sit and have a conversation with him about things in my life. I felt so close to him and I wanted to tell him things that were on my heart. But no matter how the conversation started, it ended with Dad "telling it like it is" in a very authoritative tone (commander and chief) and that was the end of the conversation. Though he was a great talker—he could talk to any one—he was not a great listener. The conversation was never two-way.

Part of the reason was a result of his extremely high level of activity. He never sat still. If we wanted to spend time with Dad, we had to do whatever he was doing. Any conversation centered on the task at hand. Whether it was fishing or fixing a car or putting new shingles on the roof, he could talk about any one of those things for hours. We all learned a lot from Dad talking about what he was doing, but we did not learn a lot about the man who was doing it. His generation was not very self-reflective, and they surely didn't talk openly about what was going on inside of them. They did what they had to do, and that was it.

The funny thing about Dad was what happened once we left home and were on our own. The gruffness ended. The military-style instructions were a thing of the past. He still was not a person you could have a heart-to-heart talk with, but he was so gentle with his words and so expressive of his love for us. I think somehow, for Dad, being responsible for his children meant he had to be very stern to make sure we were taken care of. His job, as he saw it, was to deliver us to adulthood safe and sound. That task took hard work and a lot of discipline so he took a military-like approach to parenting. But once we were on our own, his job was done and he could relax.

I remember visiting once when my youngest sister, Kari, was still living at home. She was in the bathroom at the mirror late one night and I went in to use the bathroom. (Our family lived in a very transparent way. The bathroom door was never closed unless there was company in the house or you were sick. No need to close the door. Bathroom business was public knowledge, and in a house where we all shared one bathroom it was rude to close and lock the door. To this day, unless there is company in our home, I find it hard to close the door when I use the bathroom!) As I entered the bathroom that night I could see that Kari was upset. She told me that she was upset because Dad was so gruff and almost always spoke to her in such a harsh way. She said, "He never talks to you that way. Why does he talk to me that way? He is always so lovey-dovey with you guys."

What an opportunity for me to explain to Kari the interesting phenomenon of Dad's parenting style. I assured her that our father, for whatever reason, talked to all of us the same way when we were still living at home.

For some strange reason, once we were out of the house and on our own, that changed. So different was the tone she saw him use with us in contrast to her that she could hardly believe it was true. It was true. I told her then I thought it was Dad's way of expressing his love for us and his sense of responsibility for our well-being. I think he believed he could order us into safety and happiness, and by running a "tight ship" he could prevent us from hurt and harm. Of course, we all know the concept isn't true, but every parent in some fashion wishes the same and tries to pull it off. I don't know how successful I was, but I tried to reassure her that when she was on her own, he would let go and be as gentle and soft in tone with her as he was with the rest of us—her older siblings. She would just have to be patient and wait.

I have come to understand Dad's actions are part of the legacy of the Greatest Generation. They suffered, they did their duty, and they bucked up and went on with life. Life was simple. There were good guys and bad guys. There was right and wrong. There was parent and child. And parents, especially fathers, were completely and totally responsible for the well-being of their children. From their own experience the best way to raise children to a good end was to have a military-style upbringing. There are rules and you follow them. End of discussion. They didn't talk about their feelings. They didn't talk about their doubts and fears. And they didn't indulge their children in such things. They had survived so much. They would make sure that we survived too.

However, my memories of Dad are not all "rough and gruff." I have a very powerful memory of my father showing his emotions and demonstrating his own recognition that he was not perfect.

Kari was a baby at the time, and Kathy and I, just teenagers, often took care of her. One day when we were babysitting, Kathy was carrying baby Kari down the stairs to the basement. On the way down she tripped and fell several steps to the floor, the baby falling with her. I don't remember where Dad was, but I do remember he came running when he heard Kari howling. He snatched her from Kathy, who had already checked to make sure Kari was okay, and he lit into Kathy pretty hard. How could she be so careless? She needed to be more careful. She could have killed the baby! Then he went up the stairs, checking out the baby to make sure everything was okay.

I don't remember if it was an hour later or a day later, but to me, it feels as if it happened yesterday. Kathy was in her room with the door closed. When my father knocked on the door, she let him in and she sat down on the bed. My father got down on his knees, took her hand and with tears streaming down his cheeks he apologized. He told her that he was wrong for hollering at her the way he did. He confessed that he was just scared out of his mind that the baby was hurt and he overreacted. He asked Kathy if she would forgive him. Funny. That is all I remember. I do not remember the rest of the conversation, if there was any. All I remember is that image of my father on his knees asking my sister for forgiveness. This moment was the most tender I had ever seen my father when I was still living at home. He was not the military guy or the just-do-what-I-say guy. He was a tender, loving father who had done something wrong and was man enough to admit it to his daughter. I will never forget it. All of the times he was gruff or short on conversation are overwhelmed by the vision of his humility and love.

When I was interviewing Dad and taking notes about his story, in a very roundabout way he revealed to me that he was not perfect. I had been talking to Mom, and she had told me Dad had had a little wild streak when he was younger. He was not the straight-laced preacher's boy some would expect. Mom said that he did quite a bit of drinking and carousing when she met him, which was right after he was liberated and returned from the war. Mom said that it was not until several years into their marriage that they both made a commitment to Christ and started to study the Bible and began to live their lives accordingly. I remember seeing a photo, from their early years of marriage, of Dad leaning against an automobile smoking a cigarette. He was very handsome and looked like trouble waiting to happen. A cocky grin was on his face.

But I remembered Dad telling me that after his near-death experience in the rice paddy, his life flashing before his eyes, he promised to walk the straight-and-narrow if he lived. He told me he never doubted his faith after that. I assumed any rebellious or wild oats had been sown before he went to war. So being on the investigative trail I decided to ask Dad about the slight discrepancy between his version and Mom's.

I simply stated what the discrepancy was between what Mom and he had told me. Was there a time when he had rebelled or turned away from his faith? Dad's posture became stiff, his face tightened up, and he set his jaw, as he often did when he was not pleased. I don't remember exactly what he said, but I do know I had asked a question that he didn't want to answer. There were limits to what he would talk about, and apparently I had reached those limits.

I believe the strong reaction was the remnant of a man who thought he had to do everything right and who believed loyalty and faithfulness are the highest human virtues. I think it was painful for him to remember he had made a promise in the rice paddy and that perhaps he had not kept his part of the deal as well as he might. I didn't press the issue or try to force him to talk about it. And my questioning him was not meant to embarrass or shame him, or prove him fallible. I simply wanted to hear the heart of my father speak. He was not able to do that.

No, my dad was not perfect. He was human. He had his weaknesses. He was not Mr. Perfect, but for me, he was as close as a dad could come to it.

18 That's Agape Love

My father did not seem to know how to express his love well, verbally or physically. It's funny. I never doubted that he loved me, not for a minute. As far back as I can remember I felt very loved. When I was a younger child, I don't remember him telling me that he loved me. And I don't remember cuddling or hugs and kisses as being common. But my father was very playful. His fun-loving nature expressed love to me. He loved to tease and he loved to play, so I always liked to be around him. But his affection was demonstrated mostly by what he did *for* me. And I knew that he would do *anything* for me. There was never any question about that. Dad was a doer, and he was always doing for others. I think giving and doing was the way he expressed his love most often.

After I had a home of my own, when he visited I knew I would need to have some fix-it jobs for him. He would expect it, and if I didn't have any jobs ready he would find them. He would roam, examining the door frames and windows and light switches. He would fiddle with all the appliances and make sure they were functioning as they should. He would raise the hood of the car and give it a mechanic's once-over. He would check out the siding and anything else that might need some repair or touching up. It was better if I had something for him to do or he might try to fix something I would just as soon be left alone!

There was a period in my life when I was making a lot of crafts and homemade gifts. He expressed his affection for me by bringing me all sorts of wood pieces to make plaques and wall hangings. One time, he made me a beautiful frame for my engagement picture out of a vertical slice of a tree trunk.

I still have it. It is amazing! It is a beautiful, rustic tree-bark frame with an oblong opening. I am sure it would be worth hundreds of dollars if purchased in the mountains of Colorado at some boutique in Boulder or Aspen. The frame and all the projects are how Dad expressed affection and love.

When I visited Mom and Dad's home, he seemed to be more expressive of his affection. But it was different. Dad would almost always hug me and maybe kiss me on the cheek, but his hugs were always accompanied with some roughness. It was very odd. It was almost as if he did not know how to express his love gently or that he felt that expressing affection gently was feminine and he had to prove he was a tough guy—a man. Yes, he loved me, but his love had some pretty rough edges. It was as if he loved me so much that he was afraid he might hurt me, and so he restrained himself from fully expressing it and ended up hurting me *just a little*. My father was not a violent man. I never saw him physically hurt anyone, and I never heard him raise his voice or holler. So I don't think that he was harboring some deep-seated anger that was somehow bleeding into his emotional life. It really did feel like he was *trying* to express love. It just felt rough.

I have tried to make sense of this oddity by remembering my father's hands, which were rough. I think they were large for a man his size. Maybe because he was such a skilled craftsman and so very strong, I just remember them as being large. But his fingers were big and round and tight, and his fingertips were often cracked. His knuckles always looked swollen. His hands were calloused. His fingernails were very thick and very hard. He had seriously injured a couple of fingers on one hand with a table saw, and so the muscles and tendons did not seem to work. I remember that those damaged fingers did not bend like the others. These fingers exaggerated the roughness of his hands. He was a man who used his hands his whole life, and they clearly showed the wear and tear.

Because Dad's hands were not soft and gentle, they did not express love softly and gently. His hands expressed affection roughly, stiffly. Perhaps they didn't have the sensory capability of properly judging the resulting physical experience for others.

And unfortunately his entire body followed suit. His hugs were stiff and usually accompanied with a pinch or a poke or his chin pushed into my neck or shoulder, or a slight twist of an arm. Once in a while he would actually sort of bite my shoulder—not with his bare teeth but with his lips pulled tight over his teeth so that the effect was more like being gummed than being bitten. That action too was rough and very odd. It created in me a great ambivalence. I wanted to have him hug and kiss me, but it always ended up feeling very rough and slightly dissatisfying. Remembering my father's strong, rough, and weathered hands helps me make sense of my father's roughness in expressing his affection and love for me.

There was another aspect of my father's expression of love that was rough and a little odd. My father was not much of a reader, but he was a devout Christian. He read his Bible and regularly attended church and adult Sunday school classes. He was not very sophisticated in his theological understanding. He was a meat-and-potatoes type Christian. He knew the basics very well, and he lived them.   But somewhere along the line he had learned about the different kinds of love expressed in the New Testament Bible.

In the original language of the New Testament, Greek, the word "love" can come from at least four Greek words: *phileō, storgē, eros* and *agapē*. Very simply, *phileō* love is brotherly love. Thus the city of *Phil*adelphia is the city of "brotherly love." It expresses the feelings of two people, shoulder to shoulder, working together for a common goal. *Storgē* can be thought of as "comfortable love." It is what we mean when we have an old pair of jeans that is so comfortable that we say, "I love these jeans!" *Eros* is romantic love. Thus the word *erotic* refers to the love that stirs sexual feelings and desires. It is the love of two people staring into each other's eyes and desiring to possess the other. The fourth Greek word is *agapē*, "unconditional love." It is the love that Jesus has for us. Agap*ē* is sacrificial love. Agap*ē* love gives everything with no expectation of anything in return. All but *storgē* appear in the Greek New Testament, and are all translated in English simply as "love."

Though my father probably could not have delineated or explained all four of these Greek words, he remembered the Greek word *agapē*, and he used it almost every time he said that he loved me.

I don't remember when he started, but he told my brother and all my sisters the same thing too. Dad would say, "I love you." Then he would follow up with, "That's agapē love."

We laugh when we reminisce about his strange habit. At our father's memorial service my brother, three sisters and I stood together to do the committal part of the ceremony. His body was cremated, so his remains were there in front of us in an urn. We prepared the words for his committal into the arms of the God he loved and served by using some of his own words. Then we took turns saying goodbye to Dad, saying together, Amen. The committal went like this:

All:	Jesus said
Ken:	I am the resurrection and the life
Carol:	Whoever believes in me
Kathy:	Even though they die
Kari:	They will live
Candie:	And whoever lives and believes in me
All:	Will never die.
Ken:	So it is
Carol:	In the sure and certain hope
Kathy:	Of resurrection to eternal life
All:	We commit our father's remains
Ken:	Earth to earth
Kari:	Ashes to ashes
Candie:	Dust to dust
Carol:	Looking for the blessed hope
Kari:	When our father's body
Kathy:	Will be made new
Ken:	Into the likeness of Christ
All:	The Lord and Savior whom he served and who loved him
Kari:	**That's agapē love,** and whose everlasting arms now hold him.
Ken:	The Lord greets him

All:	**Take all you want, but eat all you take** (another one of his sayings)
Ken:	Just kidding! The Lord greets him,
All:	"Well done thou good and faithful servant. Enter into the joy of the Lord."
Each one:	Goodbye, Dad.
All:	Thank you, Lord. Amen[62]

The ritual was a way for all of us to honor our father but also to acknowledge the oddity of how he expressed his love for us. Although I am grateful he said he loved me a lot more when I was older, and although I am grateful for his faith and his bedrock belief in the unconditional love of God for all of us, I always wished he would just say he loved me. I appreciate his wanting to express his unconditional love for me, but part of me just wanted to hear and feel that his affection for me was deep and full of emotion. My dad loved everyone unconditionally. Somehow I wanted him to love me *more* or at least different than everyone else. For me it felt like he was afraid to just blindly, unashamedly love me. The follow-up of "that's agapē love" always left me feeling like something of his love was being held back from me.

Intellectually, of course, I know he demonstrated his love by his actions in remarkable ways, which many children would love to have experienced from their father. But somehow for me, I longed for his unqualified love. Silly me. He was expressing Christlike love, and I just wanted plain old daddy love!

The combination of his physical roughness and always qualifying his love for me as agapē love left me feeling a little robbed of his affection, that's all. And so tears well up in my eyes even now as I tap into that longing for his unqualified love and affection. I had his unqualified support. I had his always ready helping hand. I had his tutelage in all things mechanical and practical. I had his playfulness and corny sense of humor when looking at life.

---

[62]From the memorial service committal conducted at the United Methodist Church in Rochester, Minnesota, on Tuesday, April 24, 2006.

And I had his unconditional love— agapē love. I just wish I could add to the list that I had my dad's affection. I wanted him to hug me gently and kiss my cheek and whisper that he loved me. That's all.

Since he was stolen away by Alzheimer's disease and finally stolen away by death, I am growing in my appreciation for and satisfaction with his agapē love. As I remember all the years and all the things that he said to me and did for me, my gratitude grows. And as I have traveled and studied and written and learned more about what he suffered and what he survived, I think I understand better where all that roughness in his hands and hugs came from. Four years of the constant threat of torture and death has its consequences. Four years of sheer gut-wrenching survival against all odds leaves its imprint. Four years of feeling mostly pain cannot be forgotten. Four years of the most brutal conditions imaginable would tend to leave stiff and rough edges on a person for a very long time. Perhaps, having suffered and survived, agapē love is actually as deep a love as he could offer me. This, too, is likely part of the war-forged experience of my upbringing. My father was forged by war, and so was I.

KM MARKER 112
Oil Painting, 2010

19   The "Big Boom" Ending

Dad had been a prisoner of war for forty months. He was now twenty-four years old. Some of the best years of his life had been robbed from him and brutally redirected by the Japanese. He had survived the battle for Bataan and the Death March that followed it. Sick and near death he left two POW camps, at least two work details and Bilibid Prison behind him in the Philippines. Then he somehow managed to hang on to life through the hell ships transport and now had survived more than a year of life-threatening labor and severe conditions in a POW camp and copper mine in northern Japan.

Then, "One day we woke up," my dad recalled, "and all the Japanese guards were gone." Only the Japanese camp commander was still at the camp. The commander told them, "Peace has come, but we are not best of friends yet. Be careful and have a safe trip home."[63] Later the "honcho" of the mine came to the POWs and asked, "What is the little bomb that makes a big boom?" They were told that many Japanese were dying every day. It was the first the prisoners had heard of the bombing of Hiroshima and Nagasaki.

Soon American planes were flying overhead, looking for a nearby POW camp that was known to the American military. The American plane spotted the uncharted Sendai No. 6 camp and dropped a wrench with a message tied to it, which asked the American prisoners to signal with colored flags what they needed most—food or medicine.

---

[63]Adrian R. Martin, *Brothers From Bataan* (Manhattan, Kansas: Sunflower University Press, 1992) p. 268.

The prisoners signaled that they needed both. The planes dropped a reply that the supplies would be delivered within an hour. A little while later some B29s flew over and dropped fifty-five gallon drums filled with food, candy, medicine, and clothing.

Dad remembered "The first items to parachute down from the sky were two barrels welded together. They were packed full of candy bars. 'Boy, oh boy, was that something!' "[64] Other food followed, and the men gorged themselves. Dad said, "We ate so much that we got sick. We did not know yet what was going to happen so we tried to save everything we could. I remember that I chewed gum until I had a two-inch ball and saved it just in case there wouldn't be any more."[65]

Roger Mansell, former director of the Center for Research Allied POWS Under the Japanese, sent me a military photo of Sendai No. 6 at the very time food and medicine and clothing was being dropped into the camp by parachute (See photo page 98). When he sent me the photo he said, "Your father is standing somewhere on the ground in the photograph waiting for his first meal in almost four years!"

Before the air drop, Japanese civilians gave the prisoners a Red Poll cow. The approximately five hundred prisoners butchered the cow and ate every part. The "take all you want, but eat all you take" principle went into full action.

Besides the strong desire to eat, there was also the desire to be clean. Dad said that there was an eight-foot by eight-foot tub at the camp that had been used by the Japanese soldiers for bathing. The prisoners were not allowed to use it. After the guards left the camp, the Americans took turns getting into the tub, fifteen or twenty at a time. Dad said there was so much scum on the surface of the water that the surface had to be cleaned after each group.

---

[64]Kenneth Davis, quoted in "Bataan Day," *Brainerd Daily Dispatch*, April 7, 1967, p. 6.

[65]Ibid.

Having been liberated, and after a period of time in recovery in Manila, Dad boarded a freighter for Seattle on October 6, 1945. He arrived at Ft. Louis in Seattle on October 27. The soldiers were fed very well en route. There to meet him upon his arrival were his sister Ruthie and two brothers, Francis and Art. All ex-prisoners were checked at Madigan Medical Center and then later sent to hospitals around the country, near their place of origin. Those from Minnesota were sent to Schick General Hospital in Clinton, Iowa. It was at Schick General that Dad met Alpheus (Al) Brown, from the Brainerd area, who became a good friend and who would introduce him to his future wife.

From Schick they were allowed to visit home, and Dad met Hazel at the bus depot when she came with her family to pick up Al. Because they were technically still enlisted, the men returned to Schick General and then eventually were sent to Fort Sheridan, Illinois, to be discharged.

Dad was honorably discharged on May 13, 1946. He had served the U.S. Army for five years, eight months, and seven days. His military record shows at the time of his discharge he had received the following medals (See document page 107):

- Victory Medal
- American Theater Ribbon
- Asiatic Pacific Theater Ribbon with two Bronze Battle Stars
- Nine Overseas Service Bars
- One Service Stripe
- Good Conduct Medal

My father and all the men and women who served and suffered in the WWII battle for the Philippines deserved these medals and much more. The statistics reveal the staggering truth of just how many suffered and died.

Japanese casualties: 12,000

American & Filipino casualties: 16,000

Filipino and American prisoners of war: 84,000[66]

Death rate for German POWs: 1.1 percent

Death rate for Japanese POWs: 37 percent (Bataan defenders even higher)[67]

My father was one of the fortunate who beat the three to one odds. Decades later, on May 19, 2000, the mayor of the city of Brainerd, Minnesota, proclaimed May 20, 2000, as "Kenneth Davis Day." Every day that I live, I will give thanks and celebrate the gift my father was to me and everyone who knew him. For me every day is "Kenneth Davis Day."

[66]Smurthwaite, *Pacific War Atlas*, p. 45.

[67]"Outline of Events," *Battling Bastards of Bataan*, April 4, 1998 <http://home.pacbell.net/fbaldie/Outline.html>.

20 Another Soldier's Comin' Home

When my father was diagnosed with Alzheimer's disease in 1999, my parents were living on lake property in northern Minnesota. The property required a lot of maintenance and upkeep, and the closest Davis child lived four hours away. As much as Dad and Mom loved the lake, we all knew that they could not stay, given Dad's disease. We siblings had families of our own, and no one was reasonably able to relocate to assist at their lake home.

At the time, my family and I were living in Chicago. I would have loved to have been able to insist that they relocate to Chicago and I would see to their care. But I couldn't do it. Not only because I was working full time, but at the time I knew that there was a very good chance that we would not be staying in the Chicago area. I was in the early stages of exploring a new ministry position, which could move us anywhere in the country. In fact, we did move to southern California in June 2003. I so wanted to take care of Dad, but I knew it wasn't feasible. One of the primary needs of Alzheimer's patients is routine and consistency. With all the confusion they experience, consistent surroundings are crucial, if at all possible. I wish my circumstances had been different. My inability to help provide care for my father continues to weigh on me heavily to this day.

Rochester, Minnesota, where my sister Carol lives, just four hours from Brainerd, quickly arose as the place for Mom and Dad to relocate. Everyone else lived too far away for them to stay at all in contact with friends and family in Minnesota.

And they had done a fair amount of doctoring at the Mayo Clinic in Rochester, where they would continue to receive excellent medical care. Carol had already done the lion's share of the caretaking, given the distance the rest of us lived from Minnesota. So Rochester it was. Their lake home was put on the market in January 2000 and it sold in four days. They relocated to Rochester on January 28, 2000.

Carol did a fabulous job of helping them adjust to the new senior living center they moved into. The rest of us visited as we were able, but Carol really took on their care. During our last time together as a family when Dad still recognized us, we all agreed to trust Carol with all further decisions regarding Dad's care and Mom's well-being as the disease progressed.

In June 2001 the Davis clan planned a reunion at Ken Jr.'s Colorado mountain home. It is a beautiful setting in the Collegiate Peaks of the Rockies, and the home is large enough to accommodate all of us comfortably. Carol brought her large and beautiful coach home as well. The coach was especially significant for Dad as he had already traveled in it a lot. It would provide more consistent and familiar surroundings for him both on the road and while in Colorado. It allowed him to "stay" in the same place for the entire vacation. Thank God for Carol and her husband, Bill, for providing such compassionate and generous care for our father and mother.

So the family gathered. Mom and Dad, five siblings, five spouses, all but one of the thirteen grandchildren and two great-grandchildren. We ate and played games. Dad was still able to play cards at that time. His favorite game, 500, stuck with him for a long time, although cheating increasingly became a problem. No one will ever know how much of it was due to the disease and how much was Dad's penchant for winning and taking advantage of his disease!

He was so happy to be surrounded by his family. But on occasion we would find him sitting or standing and staring off into space, clearly not present. A sort of disconnected and sad look was on his face.

Now and then he would walk up to one of us and ask a question. He came up to me and pulled at the Gordon-Conwell Seminary sweatshirt he was wearing and asked, "Are you the one that gave me this shirt?"

I responded, "Yes, Dad, I gave you that shirt." He loved that shirt. I have a picture on my dresser of him wearing it proudly. The pewter frame, given to me after his passing by one of my best friends, Marcia Agema, has a poem inscribed on it:

> Little I knew that morning, God would call your name, in life we loved you dearly, in death we do the same. It broke our hearts to lose you, you did not go alone, for part of me went with you, the day God called you home. You left us beautiful memories, your love is still our guide, and though we cannot see you, you are always by our side. Our family chain is broken, and nothing seems the same, but as God calls us one by one, the chain will link again.[68]

Another time during that reunion Dad came up to me and asked, "You are my daughter, right?" I answered, "Yes." Then he asked, "Now which ones of these kids are yours?" He and I went over the names of all the grandchildren, and I pointed out mine. He made some comment about him knowing all of the names but was just having trouble keeping it all straight.

It was there in Colorado in June 2001 we made the decision. The five of us siblings sat Mom down and told her that we cared about Dad but we also cared about her. We knew there would come a time when she could no longer care for Dad, and we didn't want her to have the burden of making that excruciating decision. With everyone present and agreeing, we decided that Carol would be the one to make the decision when the time came.

We further agreed that any and all assets needed were to be used to care for Mom and Dad without any concern for preserving anything for us. Carol would be the closest and have the best ability to make these decisions. We all promised we would not second guess her decision and trusted her to help Mom manage and use their resources accordingly. We all would support her 100 percent. I think Mom was relieved. We all were. And we were so grateful for Carol, who was willing and able to take on the immense responsibility.

---

[68]Author unknown.

The reunion was the last time we would be together when Dad remembered who we were. I realized the truth as Carol and Bill drove away in the lovely motor home, carrying Dad and Mom back to Minnesota. I knew that this time when I hugged him and said goodbye, it was a last goodbye. So as the vehicle drove down the road, I found myself standing in the Colorado Rockies crying. I had just said goodbye to my father. He was gone. Though his body would continue to live for another five years, the man that I knew, the person that was Kenneth Earl Davis, my dad, would be gone the next time I saw him. I stood and cried like a baby. I was losing my father, my teacher, my hero. I knew I would miss him. I had no idea how much.

TSGT. KENNETH E. DAVIS, CIRCA 1946
Oil Painting, 2010

21   An Angel in Tomah

The disease progressed rapidly and by December 2001 it was clear it was not safe for Mom to continue to try and care for Dad. Though eighty years old at the time, he was a very strong man and about seven inches taller than Mom, so any resistance from him or an accidental fall could result in injury to her. It was a very difficult decision to move him, but it had to be done. Once again I wished my circumstances allowed me to just drop everything and care for him, but they did not. Carol did all the foot work in investigating facilities and programs, and she found the best possible placement for him. That December he was placed in a facility especially designed for people with memory loss. It was a beautiful home-like setting with very attentive and caring staff. For the first few months every time any of us visited him, Dad begged to go home. He would say, "Please let me come home. I promise to be good." This amazing man who had taught us the essence of goodness thought he was where he was because he had been bad! Hearing him beg was so gut-wrenching! Gradually he adjusted, and as his memory continued to decline he quit asking to go home. But I will never, ever forget his face and the sound of his voice asking.

Then another juncture in his decline precipitated another move. Dad had a favorite couch in the home's common area, where he always sat. One day a female resident was sitting in his place. He pushed her out of his place and in the process she was injured. The staff could not allow him to stay. So once again Dad had to be moved.

In August 2003 Dad went to a facility in Minneapolis that specialized in assessment and care of these difficult cases. But he didn't do well there. No amount of medication that allowed him to be mobile seemed to curb his aggressive behavior and fitful sleep. He was miserable there.

We were all miserable. Again, Carol found a new place for him. It was farther away from Carol and Mom, but it was closer to Kari, our youngest sister, so there would be more possibility for visits and sharing in his care. All his years of suffering and service to his country would now pay dividends. Dad was going to be cared for at the Veteran's Hospital in Tomah, Wisconsin, which had a specialized unit for residents with memory loss. I was skeptical, because in my ministry career I had seen some pretty horrible VA facilities. But I trusted Carol, and we had all agreed to support her in these difficult decisions. It turned out to be the perfect place for Dad. He was extremely well cared for in his final days.

Every day I thought of my dad, I prayed that someone would give him the love and care that I so desperately wanted to give him and could not. It was a bold prayer because I know for a fact that often much of the staff in these kinds of facilities have high turnover and are poorly paid, yet they have very difficult and demanding jobs. But I kept praying. I knew that my two sisters who lived within a couple of hours were seeing him as regularly as they could, and Carol was bringing my mom to see him too. But I wondered *what kind of people are providing daily care for Dad?* I prayed that somehow God would send him an angel to love him.

Through a very roundabout way I found out that my prayer was answered. The following email from my brother says it all.

> **From**: *Ken Davis*
> **Sent**: *Thursday, June 29, 2006 9:50 AM*
> **To**: *Carol Klepper; Kari Harsch, Candie Blankman; Kathy Colebank, Diane*
> **Subject**: *FW: Your Dad*

To my dearest sisters,

While speaking at a conference at Willow Creek, a beautiful young woman came up to me and asked that I provide a signature for her mother.

She went on to inform me that her mother had cared for Dad during the last months of his life. I must admit I lost it for a few minutes. After regaining my composure, I wrote the sweet angel a note thanking her for her compassion.

This is the email I received in return. I thought it might bless you to know that Dad was loved by more than just his family and that his last days were blessed by the presence of this kind of love.

Also thought you might like to let her know your appreciation.

Ken

P.S. I have underlined a couple of important passages in the communication.

--Original Message--
From: Karalyn Renaud
Sent: Tuesday, June 27, 2006 11:35 PM
To: Ken Davis
Subject: Your Dad

Dear Ken,
I am responding to the request you made of my daughter during the THWONK! Session at the Willow Arts Conference held in Chicago 6/15-16. I first met your father in May 2004, as I became employed at the Tomah VAMC. It was not until nearly 1 ½ years into my employment there that I made the connection between you and your father. Another staff member informed me that his son was some sort of speaker and there were tapes in the closet.

One evening while working the evening shift I kept your dad up a bit past his bedtime along with a couple other residents and my co-worker to view one of your videos.

I chose the one where you honored him for his military sacrifice. Although he was incapable of effective verbal communication, <u>when you appeared on the screen, he raised his right arm and said, "That's my son</u>." My heart leapt as he sat intently throughout the duration of that video—alert and attentive.

Having learned a bit of his prior POW status from staff, I had a great sense of awe and honor and would often desire to know more of who he was.

Despite his inability to communicate, I was determined to provide his care despite his protestations and resistance, with a desire to demonstrate love and tenderness. <u>I wanted so that he should know safety, comfort, and tenderness as gratitude for all he had suffered for me and mine.</u>

His eyes said so very much. Sometimes there was a faraway gaze, other times a sparkle and yet other times as I kissed his head and whispered a blessing in his ear, there seemed to be a release. A gentle quietness would come over him and I knew, he knew, that his Father and I loved him.

I have not grieved the loss of others as I did your father. Truly, Ken, I have never known such privilege and honor in serving anyone in the capacity of a nursing assistant until I met your father.

My husband and children have since come to know who your father was and sorrowed with you at the time of your loss. I have met your mom on two occasions and two of your sisters. I would be equally blessed to someday meet you. You delighted my daughter at the conference—and be assured, I scolded her for asking what language your handwriting was written in. She gets that from her father.

I shall treasure your note to me.
In Christ Jesus, Karalyn Renaud[69]

---

[69]Email from Ken Davis Jr., June 29, 2006. Printed by permission of Karalyn Renaud.

God in His grace and mercy answered my prayer. He sent an angel to the Tomah VA Hospital to love and care for my father. Her name was Karalyn Renaud.

The suffering of my dad's imprisonment and the sadness of my father's final years left its mark on all of us. But so did his humor and positive outlook. Our brother, Ken, seemed to get a double portion of the humor. He has made a very comfortable living out of his gift of humor, traveling extensively doing comedy concerts and writing several books as an inspirational humorist. Even in these sad days of disease, death, and loss, he helped us get through with his unrelenting wit. In case you didn't catch it, the humor is in the first sentence underlined in the email (go back and check). I really appreciated him highlighting the desire of the woman to serve our father for all he had sacrificed for her and her family. But underlining the part about Dad recognizing him in the video when he no longer recognized any of us? This was too much. He was using humor to skewer his sisters. Dad always did like him best. Why? He had the right body parts. (That's my story and I'm sticking to it.)

22 Dream Accomplished

More than a year has already passed since I visited the places where my father was a prisoner of war in World War II. Since that time I have finished several oil paintings and am about to complete the written account of his life and my attempt to understand it. It has been a roller coaster of emotion. I have sat with the text and laughed out loud, and I have also cried. I have been totally consumed in creating canvas representations, and I have been paralyzed and unable to lift a brush for fear that I would not do justice to what I have learned and experienced.

More than twenty years ago it began with a simple desire to talk to my dad about what he had experienced. The simple desire quickly became a need to record it so that others could have the privilege of knowing what I was hearing. The need developed into a dream. The dream was to research and travel in order to fill in some of the empty spaces and to corroborate my father's memory when possible and correct it if necessary. The research was aided immensely by my husband, Drew, who is much better at finding and keeping details than I am. The travel was a dream I did not dare to express because it seemed beyond our means.

Thanks to the Lily Foundation and their vision of encouraging and supporting ministers, my dream came true. Thanks to my congregation, First Presbyterian Church of Downey, California, who gave me the freedom to follow the dream and granted me the three-month sabbatical to travel, write, and to paint. I knew when I began the odyssey that my father was a formidable influence in my life. And I knew some of the forces that drove that influence.

But I had no idea how much he had influenced me. I knew only a fraction of the reality of war that forged that influence. My father, along with hundreds of thousands of other WWII veterans, was indelibly imprinted by the war to save democracy and the free world. Young and enthusiastic, they enlisted during hard times at home—the Great Depression and its aftermath—and had little sense of what they were getting into. My father wanted to travel to where it was warm and beautiful. A map of the Philippine Islands and the vivid description of an army recruiter convinced him that was where he should go.

But what he experienced there, no map or recruiter or basic training could prepare him for. Although he was raised in a family of fifteen children and knew relative poverty, the deprivation of almost four years as a prisoner of war under the Japanese taught him things about life and death that he could not have learned any other way.

My father learned to use his stubborn determination to survive and to thrive. He learned to rise above the obstacles and life-threatening challenges to see possibilities that could only be seen with the heart. He learned to lean on and trust the faith he received as a child in order to overcome whatever life brought his way. My father learned to appreciate the simplest things in life and to share them with everyone. In stark contrast to how he had been treated, he became a consummate helper of others. He learned to enjoy life and make people laugh. Though brutalized and deprived by his captors, he became a person of immense hospitality and was generous to a fault. Even though surrounded by hatred and evil for four years, he developed into a man who loved others deeply and prayed daily to be a good man, with God's help.

He saw so much inhumanity, how did he become a human being so kind? Though effectively silenced for all those years, he rediscovered his gregarious self and used his charm and gift of gab to share the love of God boldly with virtually everyone he met. He was not perfect, but he was on a journey toward Christlikeness that transformed him day by day into more and more of what God calls men to be.

This is the man that influenced my life more than any other. He is the man I followed as a youngster. With him I climbed roofs, peered into engines, tore things apart, and put them back together again. This man taught me to draw and shade letters. He is the one who taught me to use my muscles and my brain and to trust my gut. By his example he showed me what hard work looked like and how an honest person behaved and spoke. Through his simple child-like faith he taught me to value God's Word, care for God's people, and to share God's love with everyone. He taught me as much about being a pastor as did my seminary education. Living with him I had years of practical internship before I ever knew I was headed for the ministry.

The loud voice and strong, weathered hands scared me as a child, but as an adult reminded me of constant and steadfast love. And both softened as he got older—his voice and his hands.

His stubborn determination and unrelenting positive view of life forged in me a person who, though often disappointed, never gives up. These strengths created in me a person and a pastor who believes there is good to be found in every person and every situation. Although he often said, "Do as I say, not as I do," he lived in such a way that I can only hope to do as he did. And one of the greatest surprises and joys I discovered regarding his influence on me was my drawing and painting. I had not taken up a pencil or paintbrush for more than thirty-five years. Something within called me to not only write but to draw and paint. My first oil painting was a portrait of my father in his later years (See painting page 186). And as I began to paint, I rediscovered the creative and artistic gifts he passed on to me. The rediscovered artistic vein in me has been a blessing as it has softened the voice and hands of this hard-driving, stubborn, verbose person and pastor. I am a recovering workaholic, and to a large degree it's because of these tendencies I have neglected the gift of art for, oh, so long. My father gave me this, too.

Dad did not become a multicultural person by choice. He was plunged into it. His military and war experiences placed in front of him people from all over the world—some for good, some for ill. But he learned through it all that race and color or shape and size do not make the heart of a person. His openness to others so very different from him, and potentially threatening to him, was perhaps his greatest gift of all to me.

My life has been so enriched by openness to others. One of my very best friends as a child was Juanita Harding. She was a Native American and a foster child of a family in the Kelsey Community Church we attended when we lived in northern Minnesota. We were like two peas in a pod. It was not until fifteen years later that I discovered there was racial tension between whites and Native Americans. I attended the Bemidji State University in northern Minnesota located near several Indian reservations. I remember hearing someone talking disparagingly about Indians, and for the first time I realized that Juanita was different from me and that some people very much disliked the Native Americans.

My father was the friend of the mentally challenged residents of the hospital where he worked. He brought them home for picnics and parties. He and I taught a Sunday school class designed just for them. It wasn't until my senior year in high school, when I saw the harassment of a mentally challenged young man who attended our school, that I realized these people were different from me, too, and that many people disliked them as well.

And my father talked to everyone. Store clerk, policeman, pedestrian, young mother strolling a baby—it didn't matter. He was a friend of all and could strike up a conversation anywhere, anytime. I inherited that nature from him often to the chagrin of my husband and children who are kept waiting when I get caught up in conversation.

I never heard him give excuses about why he couldn't do something. I only saw him try. And I rarely saw him fail. He raised me to believe I could do anything too. I could be the president of Student Council even though only one other girl had ever done it in the history of my high school. I could be a pastor even though I had never seen or heard a woman pastor in my entire life.

I could camp outside in the dead of winter in the Boundary Waters of northern Minnesota. I could get a job managing a restaurant even though I had only been a waitress and hostess before.

With the right tools I could figure out how to fix things on my own, most of the time. I did not need to find someone else to do it. I could trust people. I could help people. I could enjoy life without a lot of money. I could travel the world by myself and not be afraid. I could be both strong and sensitive. I could trust God.

These lessons my father taught me. I learned from living with him, from listening to him and from studying, writing and painting about his life. My life is an image of what it means to be the child of one of the Battling Bastards of Bataan. I am who I am because I was raised in a family whose father was a soldier and a prisoner of war. I am forged by war.

KENNETH E. DAVIS, CIRCA 1995
Oil Painting 2009

Appendix 1: Kenneth Earl Davis: Basic Information and Military Chronology

Early Years
March 24, 1921
- Born in Barrows, Minnesota, to Lester and Sara Davis

Spring 1936
- Finished ninth grade, Pillager High School, Pillager, Minnesota
- Joined CCC Camp in Wilton, Minnesota

Enlistment
September 7, 1940
- Enlisted, private, 31st Infantry Regiment, U.S. Army
- One month training: student radio operator
- Three months: fixed-station radio operator, private first class
- Staff sergeant: regimental draftsman
- Drawing plans for carpentry and keeping and correcting maps for military maneuvers, Fort Snelling, St. Paul, Minnesota

Military Assignment
November 17, 1940
- Shipped to Philippine Islands
- First Command Post, regimental draftsman
- Cuartel de Espana, Quartermaster Headquarters Company

War Begins
December 7, 1941
- Pearl Harbor

December 8, 1941
- Troops in Philippines told they had about "42 hours" till Japanese Army could exert significant pressure
- Clark Airfield, Luzon, Philippine Islands bombed by Japanese
- Later sent to Olongapo Marine Base, west coast Bataan Peninsula, Philippine Islands, to check for anything useful

- Later sent to Mariveles, southern tip of Bataan Peninsula, Philippine Islands (acc. to Robert Hudson)[70] to set up command post and communication system.

December 24, 1941
- MacArthur orders general retreat to Bataan—U.S. and Filipino troops began two-week withdrawal from Manila to Bataan Peninsula

January 2, 1942
- Japanese occupy Manila
- Later Ken ordered to Orani, northern Bataan Peninsula
- Later helped to set up several lines of defense as the Japanese army advanced from Manila to Bataan

January 24, 1942
- Withdrawal to second line of defense from Bagac to Orion, Bataan Peninsula

February 22, 1942
- General Edward King takes command of troops on Bataan
- Later withdrawal to third line of defense Ken in a jeep accident; ends up in a hospital overnight

Prisoner of War in the Philippines
April 9, 1942
- Gen. Edward King surrenders Bataan at Limay
- Ken and two other soldiers (Jackson and Weber) try to make it on their own in the jungle
- Weber later joined an American contingent surrendering

April 12, 1942
- Ken and Jackson hid guns in a tree trunk
- Ken and Jackson picked up by Japanese in American jeep
- Began the Bataan Death March, 60-66 miles to San Fernando, Pampanga, Luzon, Philippine Islands

---

[70]Robert Hudson's father was also a POW of the Japanese in WWII, and Robert has done extensive research on the subject. My brother, Ken Davis Jr., met Robert at one of Ken's comedy concerts, and as a result Ken and I both attended the first annual Convention of the Descendants of the American Defenders of Bataan and Corregidor.

April 14-26, 1942

- Boxcars to Capas, Tarlac, Luzon, Philippine Islands
- March again six miles to Camp O'Donnell
- Arrived April 24

June 2-6, 1942

- Taken by truck to Cabanatuan, Nueva, Ecija, Luzon, Philippine Islands
- Limay Bridge Detail, southern end of Bataan

November 1942

- Clark Airfield Detail, Luzon, Philippine Islands
- More "civilized" and Japanese guards were "decent"

Date Unknown

- Bilibid Prison Hospital, Manila, Luzon, Philippine Islands for one month

Prisoner of War in Japan

August 25, 1944

- Put on the hell ship *Noto Maru* (1,035 men), Manila Harbor

August 27, 1944

- Ship left
- Last ship to leave that was not torpedoed/sunk
- 3 left after, all sunk, 3,000 U.S. POWs lost

August 31, 1944

- Stopped in Takao, Formosa

September 1, 1944

- Left Takao

September 5, 1944

- Arrived Moji, Japan

September 6, 1944

- Ferry to Shimonoseki, Japan
- Train to Tokyo—on the way 500 dropped off at various camps

September 9, 1944

- 535 arrived Sendai No. 6, Hanawa Camp, near present day Kazuno City, Akita Prefecture, Honshu Island, Japan

- Walked 1.5 miles to Osarizawa, small town nearby with newly constructed POW camp
- Forced labor in Mitsubishi copper mine "horrific" conditions and "sadistic and inhumane" guards

Liberation Begins

August 6, 1945

- First atomic bomb dropped on Hiroshima, Japan

August 9, 1945

- Second atomic bomb dropped on Nagasaki, Japan

August 10, 1945

- First air raid over Hanawa, Kazuno City, Japan

August 15, 1945

- Japan surrendered
- August 20, 1945
- "Peace Speech" delivered

August 21, 1945

- Supply drops began

September 10, 1945

- Commandeered train/Ordered to leave

September 14, 1945

- Arrived Shiogama, Japan

September 15, 1945

- Barge to hospital ship *Rescue*

September 16, 1945

- Arrived by troop transport to Yokohama, Japan

September 19, 1945

- Sailed for Manila, Luzon, Philippine Islands

September 26, 1945

- Arrived in Manila, 29th Replacement Camp

October 8, 1945

- Boarded Dutch ship, *Clip Fontaine*
- Shipped Ft. Lewis/Madigan Medical Center, Seattle, Washington

October 27, 1945

- Arrived Seattle, Washington

November 1945
- Sent to Schick General Hospital, Clinton, Iowa
- Met Al Brown and saw picture of Al's sister Hazel

Date Unknown
- Picked up by family (met Hazel), Brainerd, Minnesota

February 20, 1946
- Triple wedding; married Hazel Irene Brown, Nisswa, Minnesota
- Honeymooned in Detroit, Michigan

May 13, 1946
- Discharged at Ft. Sheridan, Illinois, north of Chicago, rank technical sergeant.

Medals
- Victory Medal
- American Theater Ribbon
- Asiatic Pacific Ribbon
- 2 Bronze Stars
- 9 Overseas Service Bars
- 1 Service Stripe
- Good Conduct Medal
- POW Medal

Post Military Work and Life
1946-1954
- Lived in the Brainerd, Minnesota area
- Blau-Gas, Brainerd, Minnesota
- Alderman-Magham Hardware Store, Brainerd, Minnesota
- Billy Graham Soft Water, Brainerd, Minnesota

1954-1966
- Lived in Sax, Minnesota (address was Zim, Minnesota)
- Mesabi Iron Mines, Eveleth, Minnesota
- Taconite Mines, Silver Bay, Minnesota
- Gino Paulucci Research Farm, Zim, Minnesota

1966-1974
- Lived in St. Peter, Minnesota
- St. Peter State Hospital, 1966-1974

1974–2000
- Lived in Nisswa, Minnesota
- Brainerd State Hospital, 1974-1986

March 23, 1986
- Retired

November 1999
- Diagnosed with Alzheimer's disease

January 28, 2000
- Ken and Hazel moved to Shorewood Senior Living Center, Rochester, Minnesota

May 20, 2000
- Mayor of Brainerd Minnesota, proclaimed "Kenneth Davis Day" (See document page 108)

December 4, 2001
- Ken moved to Sunrise, Memory Loss Facility, Rochester, Minnesota

September 1, 2003
- Ken moved to Bethesda Sunrise, St. Paul, Minnesota

October 23, 2003
- Ken moved to VA Hospital, Tomah, Wisconsin

April 18, 2006
- Kenneth Earl Davis died

April 24, 2006
- Memorial Service, Rochester, Minnesota

April 26, 2006
- Burial, Fort Snelling National Cemetery, St. Paul, Minnesota (See photo page 100)

Appendix 2: Camp O'Donnell Conditions

1. O'Donnell got its name from a family of early Spanish settlers in the late 1800's. It has been used to hold soldiers ever since its founding and, prior to hostilities, construction was being done starting in September 1941 to make the camp permanent. Construction work ceased in mid-December 1941 when the troops were sent north to defend against the December 23 Japanese landings.

2. Called lugao by the Filipinos, The thin watery soup was a main staple for the POWs during captivity.

3. Rules laid down by the Japanese camp commandant were:

   The Japanese army does not recognize rank of prisoners of war.

   Prisoners will salute all Japanese officers and soldiers while wearing headgear and bow appropriately when not.

   Daily check-ups will be made [accountability of personnel].

   Men will not leave the barracks between the hours of 7:00 p.m. and 6:40 a.m.

   None will approach nearer than three meters to the fence surrounding the compound.

   Water will be economized.

   Only sponge baths are permitted.

   No smoking within twenty feet of a building.

   All borrowed articles from the Japanese will be carefully accounted for.

   Anyone disobeying orders or trying to escape will be shot to death.

   All requests should be sent through proper channels.

4. The first act by the captors, after the commandant's address, was to shake down every officer and enlisted prisoner. If any possessions

remained after the Death March, all prisoners were stripped of their blankets, pencils, pens, lighters, knives, surgical equipment, paper, and tobacco products. Almost everything of value was taken from the prisoners, leaving them with nothing but their canteens and mess kits.

5.   Author Olson writes in *O'Donnell*, "Of all the buildings in the camp, none was regarded by the captives with such awe and fatal fascination as was the Hospital... if it could be called a 'hospital,' it was merely a place for men to go to die." Master Sergeant Gaston, who saw the ward in July 1942, had this graphic description: "The men in the ward were practically nothing but skin and bones and they had open ulcers on their hips, on their knees and on their shoulders... maggots were eating on the open wounds. There were blow flies... by the millions... men were unable to get off the floor to go to the latrine and their bowels moved as they lay there." Of all those that had it the most difficult was the American placed in charge, Capt. John Rizzolo, who was the officer in charge of the ward from its creation until early May 1942. With minimal supplies and little support from Japanese captors, Rizzolo did the best he possibly could do.

Note: Tarlac prison camp was in existence for only a few months- from May 20, 1942, to August 17, 1942. It was used for high-ranking officers, including General Wainwright, four major generals, ten brigadier generals, one hundred six colonels, and a number of orderlies. After the fall of Corregidor, General Wainwright and five of his staff officers were taken to Lamao on the Bataan Peninsula on May 7, 1942. From there the general and his staff were moved to Station KZRH in Manila to broadcast the surrender order to the other commands located throughout the islands.

While in Manila, Wainwright sent a letter to General Homma requesting that he send a radio message to President Roosevelt, in his name, asking for a ship to be dispatched at once to the Philippines with food, clothing, and medical supplies, for American and Filipinos were dying at a rate of 300 a day at

O'Donnell. No message was sent. On June 9, 1942, the Japanese captors informed Wainwright that his high command had ceased to exist and then moved him and his staff to the prison camp for senior officers in Tarlac. Wainwright and other senior officers, like General King, stayed at Tarlac until August 12, 1942, when they were loaded on a prison ship and were transported to Karenko in Formosa.

Death Becomes an Everyday Occurrence

One of the first formations we saw as we were marching into O'Donnell, was a funeral detail of men with picks and shovels carrying crude litters of dead as they moved slowly, under Nip guard, toward the burial ground. We were to see the same sight each day during our stay there, but I am sad to say that the size of the parties and the number of litters were always on the increase.

Many men had arrived at the end of the Death March so far gone that they never recovered. There were many cases of malaria for which there was no medicine, and there were many new cases of dysentery occurring each day that we were at the camp. It was not uncommon to find a few men dead in barracks when we got up in the morning. Even though medicine soon became practically nonexistent, General King established a hospital under the care of the American personnel in camp. He directed that something could be done for them because he hoped to reduce the alarming increase in infectious diseases.

During the first few days after the sick were collected and brought into the hospital, the starving hospital personnel were very busy for not only were there many dead and dying men in the hospital, but a number of them crawled outside to die, and a few bodies were found under the building when the odor of decay brought out searching parties. The hospital became known as the "Pest House," into which many entered but few returned.

Sometime later, after we had received orders to move, a friend of mine insisted that I go through the hospital to see for myself the terrible conditions there which he stated were beyond description. I had to go tell Griff goodbye anyway, for malaria had laid him low, so I made the visit. Griff was in one of the cleaner rooms, among men who did not have dysentery and who were strong enough to visit the latrine. Although all the patients were sleeping on the floor, they were as comfortable as they would have been in barracks. All of the rooms were filled with large green mosquito nets of squad size, large enough for eight or more men to lie without crowding, protected from the attacks of mosquitoes by night and flies by day. We told Griff that we expected him to join us soon, which he did, he being one of the small numbers to survive the Pest House.

After leaving Griff, we entered what must have been the dysentery ward for the floor was covered with emaciated bodies in various stages of undress, lying in their own filth. I do not believe any one of them could have stood on his feet, and most of them did not appear to be aware of where they were, nor of the seriousness of their condition. There were no bedpans but, if there had been, the men could not have used them. Not only were the clothes of the men, but the blankets and the floor around them soiled. The physical state of the men was so pitiable, the living conditions so frightful, and the odor so overwhelming, that I could not take it anymore.

Outside, one of the doctors told me that there had been more than a thousand deaths in the first forty days at the camp and, furthermore, if that rate continued the last man of us would be dead before the year had passed by. The death rate among Filipinos in the southern part of the camp was considerably higher than in ours, but I have forgotten the figures. There were so many deaths that the Nips insisted on the burials being made in mass graves, which was a practical solution to the problem, there being so few men who were capable of performing hard labor.

Prisoner-Captor Relationships

The Nips (term used at that time) issued an order that there would be no association or communications between the Americans in the north part of the camp and the Filipinos in the south part. The Nip section being in between the two prisoner sections, the order was pretty well enforced, but the work parties of Americans and Filipinos met frequently at the burial ground, at the ration warehouses, and at other work projects.

Whenever the work parties met there were always many questions asked by both groups. We learned that the death rate among the Filipinos was even higher than among the Americans. We also learned by reports and observations that the attitude of the Japanese toward the Americans differed from their attitude toward the Filipinos. That was understandable in view of the fact that Americans were permanent captives whereas the Filipinos, after indoctrination, were expected to return home and assist the Filipino people [in becoming] loyal serfs of Japan.

The object of Japan being to develop the Philippines into a vassal state, it was difficult to understand why the Japanese were so openly contemptuous, cruel, and arbitrary in their treatment of the Filipinos. The Nips made no attempt to conceal that they considered the Filipino soldiers the scum of the earth, unworthy of any respect or consideration.

While the same cruelty and starvation diet was meted out to the Americans and Filipinos alike, the Nips could not conceal a certain respect and admiration for the American soldier which was in sharp contrast to their attitude towards the Filipino soldier of who they considered no soldier at all.

NOTE: Credit for this information goes to Colonel Irvin Alexander, author of "Surviving Bataan and Beyond," published from his manuscripts made in 1949.

Appendix 3: Camp Cabanatuan Conditions

In order to completely segregate Americans from their Filipino comrades, the Japanese began transferring the Americans to the three Cabanatuan prison camps in late May 1942. The town of Cabanatuan, or Cabanatuan City, is located on the Pampanga River, forty miles from Fort Stotsenburg and one hundred miles north of Manila. There were three camps at Cabanatuan numbered 1, 2, and 3. Camp No. 1 was approximately four miles to the east of Cabanatuan City. Camp No. 2 was four miles farther on in the same direction, and Camp No. 3 was six miles past No. 2. A small dirt road connected the two camps at No. 2 and No. 3. In addition to those arriving from O'Donnell were many of the Americans in Bataan field hospitals who were brought to No. 3 in late May 1942. Shortly thereafter, the men who surrendered at Corregidor also arrived at No. 3. When No. 3 was filled, the remaining POW's from Corregidor were placed in No. 2. When no water supply was found at No. 2, those in No. 2 were transferred to No. 1 in early June and No. 2 was maintained in the future mostly for naval personnel. In late October 1942, No. 3 was permanently closed and the prisoners located there were moved to No. 1.

The Cabanatuan "hospital" was first opened in June 1942 under the command of Colonel James Gillespie. At the hospital there were thirty wards (made to hold forty soldiers each), often holding up to 100 patients. In each ward were upper and lower decks made of bamboo slats. Each patient was allotted a two by six foot space. The seriously ill were kept on the lower deck. Fenced off from the hospital was a quarantined area containing about ten wards, called the dysentery section. Within the dysentery section was a building missed when the wards were numbered. Later, it was called the "zero" ward (due to the fact that one had "zero" chance of leaving it alive), and served as a place to put seriously ill or dying patients.

Camp No.3 was divided into three distinct groups by the Japanese, mostly for control purposes. The overall American commander at the camp, until he was sent to Bilibid Prison on August 30, 1942, and then to Karenko on September 27, 1942, was Colonel Napolean Boudreau, the former commander of Subic Bay Harbor defenses. Replacing Boudreau was Lieutenant Commander Curtis T. Beecher, a Marine. The commander of Camp No. 1 was Colonel Leo Paquet (USMA 1919) Colonel Armand Hopkins (USMA 1925) was the commander of Group No. 2. When many of the prisoners were sent away to become slave laborers for the Japanese, the groups were consolidated into one group, with Paquet in command and Hopkins as his executive officer. Numerous changes in command occurred over the years that the prisoners occupied the various Cabanatuan camps but, for the most part, the chain of command noted above was in place while Alexander was a captive at Cabanatuan.

There was a very organized underground system at Cabanatuan. Food and money were smuggled into the camp on a daily basis. The principal organizers of the smuggling activities were two American women, Margaret Utinsky ("Miss U") and Claire Philips ("Highpockets"). Both were the wives of American soldiers who died in Cabanatuan during the summer of 1942 and both had avoided confinement in the civilian internment camp at Santo Tomas in Manila. The underground organization received help from local merchants, farmers, and businessmen who provided "baked cookies," or in other words, produced other foods, medicines, notes, and money to the prisoners. A Filipina mestiza, Evangeline Neibert ("Sassie Suzie") carried the "cookies" by train from Manila to the town of Cabanatuan, where she delivered them to the market. Naomi Flores ("Looter"), a licensed vegetable peddler, hid the loot in the bottom of rice sacks and took them to the camp. Once or twice a week, the rice detail from the camp picked up the sacks of rice and took them to the mess hall, where the goods were removed and delivered to one of six officers designated as "helpers." The helpers then delivered the goods to the beds of those requesting the notes and/or goods.

Lieutenant Colonel Harold K. Johnson, an infantry officer in charge of the Cabanatuan commissary, estimated that while the underground was in operation, he spent nearly one and one-half million pesos on food and other items with and apparent income of only one-half million. On May 3, 1944, the Japanese put an end to the underground operations when a group of men were compromised in Manila. Several "ring leaders" and American sympathizers were severely punished, including imprisonment and execution.

The camp commandant was Lieutenant Colonel Masao Mori, who operated a bicycle shop in Manila when the war began. He was nicknamed "Blood" and "Bamboo Mori" by the prisoners. Mori, who was in charge of both Camp No.1 and No. 3, chose to live at No. 3 until he moved to No. 1 in September

1942. He and another guard, Kasayama Yoshikichi, who the prisoners called "Slime," were the terror of the camp. Blood and Slime were punished after the war as war criminals. Blood was hanged and Slime got a life sentence. In late October 1942 Mori was replaced (after Camp No. 3 was closed and all prisoners were transferred to No. 1) by Major Iwanaka. Iwanaka was quite old for a major and paid no attention to the goings-on in the camp. In June 1944 Iwanaka was relieved by Major Takasaki, who ruled the camp with an iron fist.

First lieutenant was Oiagi, the camp quartermaster. He was tall and had played on the Japanese Davis Cup team in America. Unlike most of the prison guards, Oiagi was relatively fair and pleasant to the POWs.

The prisoners had many "affectionate" nicknames for their guards: Big Stoop, Little Speedo, Air Raid, Laughing Boy, Donald Duck, Many Many, Beetle Brain, Fish Eyes, Web Foot, Hammer Head, and Hog Jaw were just a few names known to most prisoners at Cabanatuan. Urban McVey, in Martin's *Brothers from Bataan,* said that "Two of the main guards were 'Big Speedo' and 'Little Speedo.' They were called that because if you were too slow in your work they would yell and holler 'Speedo'. 'Big Speedo' didn't beat up the prisoners. 'Little Speedo' did, and he was much bossier than 'Big Speedo.'"

The American prisoners had been severely warned upon entering any prison camp that an attempt to escape would result in death by firing squad. Despite the warnings, a handful of escape attempts from Cabanatuan occurred in the early days of incarceration. If the escapees were captured they were usually tortured and shot to death while other POWs were forced to look on. To prevent any more escape attempts, the Japanese captors initiated what were called "Shooting Squads" or "Blood Brothers." Each POW was assigned to a group of ten. If anyone in that group escaped, the other nine would be shot. When it came to the deed, the Japanese often had mixed feelings about whether to actually shoot the helpless hostages or not. Sometimes they did, sometimes they didn't, but one could never feel any confidence about the matter. Author Thomas, in *As I Remember,* writes, "You can believe that each man knew where his blood brothers were most of the time and especially at night." Because of the danger to those in the camp, the American leadership took extra precautions by imposing additional rules to prevent escape attempts and to prevent the perception (which had occurred more often than not) of a POW trying to escape. For instance, the Japanese rule was to stay within ten feet of the fence. The American leaders made it thirty. In addition, a walking, unarmed patrol of POWs was formed to watch for anything suspicious. The patrol wore white armbands with MP printed on them.

During the first eight months of camp in Cabanatuan, deaths totalled approximately 2,400. Some 30 to 50 skeletons, covered by leathery skin, were buried in common graves each day. The Japanese issued documents certifying that each death was caused by malaria, beriberi, pellagra, diphtheria, in fact, anything but the real cause–starvation and malnutrition. Death hit the youngest men the hardest. Of the men who died during July 1942 at Camp No. 1, 85 per cent were under 30. Ten per cent of the enlisted men died, compared with only 4 per cent of the officers.

Addendum:

Following is a report of Colonel Webb E. Cooper's "Medical" Department Activities in the Philippines from 1941 to May 6, 1942:

"Each day an attempt was made to clear each barracks of the dying. They were removed to 'zero' ward, laid on the bare floor entirely naked. These patients usually were profoundly emaciated, in fact, little better than skeletons with a feeble spark of life. Heroic corpsmen and doctors did what they could to alleviate the indescribable conditions. They tied grass onto sticks and attempted to cleanse the floors. They used the same method of cleansing the body. Occasionally a big puddle of rainwater would provide enough water to wash the floor. At the time the use of the regular water supply system was strictly forbidden by the Japanese. The few laymen who saw these conditions were utterly horrified. Even the Japanese doctors would not enter these wards and the Japanese staff at Headquarters gave it a wide berth. ".

NOTE: Credit for the information goes to Colonel Irvin Alexander, author of "Surviving Bataan and Beyond," published from his manuscripts made in 1949.

For more information on these camps check on the Biographies and Account Link as well as the Recommended Reading Link.

Appendix 4: Bilibid Prison

"Bilibid Prison was a sprawling seventeen-acre quadrangle (a penitentiary the size of five city blocks) in the center of Manila… Behind its high stone walls, topped with barbed wire, were long one-story cell blocks and barred dormitories radiating out form a central rotunda and watchtower… It was an ancient prison, built by the Spanish in 1865… roughly half the compound, was a central hospital for all prisoners of war in the islands… roofs leaked… almost everything else inside the crumbling prison was rusted and rotting or in disr`epair.[71]

"…overwhelmed by the number of patients, the doctors mostly warehoused the sick…. the Japanese brought in a group of Navy doctors and corpsmen led by Commander Lea B. "Pappy" Sartin and his chief of surgery, Lieutenant Commander Thomas H. Hayes. Sartin… took a look around at the 'filthy and degrading hell hole' and immediately ordered his 26 doctors, 11 dentists, and 165 corpsmen, pharmacist's mates, and orderlies to scrub it down and effect repairs. Pappy Sartin set down the rules, but Hayes was the hospital's real ramrod. A day or two after he arrived, he visited each ward to see what was waiting for him.

"[*Hayes, 'Notebook,' July 4, 1942*] A walk thru the length of the wards, each holding about eighty cadaverous animals that once were men, is one of the most desperate, heartrending sights conceivable… "

---

[71]A description of Bilibid from *Tears in the Darkness* by Michael and Elizabeth Norman, New York: Farrar, Straus, Giroux, 2009, pp. 266-67.

Appendix 5: The "Peace" Speech

The "Peace" Speech by Lieutenant Asaka given on August 20 at 9:30 a.m. to announce the end of the war. The speech was given in Japanese but translated into English and later posted and many copied it.

> Peace, peace comes to all the world again. It is great pleasure for me, to say nothing of you, to announce it for all of you now. The Japanese Empire acknowledges the terms of suspension of hostilities as given by the American Government even though these two nations do not still reach the best agreement of a truce. As a true friend from now on I am going to do my best in the future for the convenience of your life in this camp because of having been able to get friendly relations between them, and also the Japanese have decided their own Nation's Policy for your Nation. Therefore, I hope you will keep a comfortable daily life by the orders of your own officers from today while you are staying here. All of you will surely get much gladness in returning to your own lovely country. At the same time one of my wishes for you is this: your health and happiness will call upon you and your life henceforth will grow up happier and better than before by the honor of your own country. In order to guard your life I have been endeavoring in ability. There you will please cooperate with me in anything more than usual, I hope. I enclose the statement in letting your honor again. The peace already has come.[72]

---

[72] Adrian R. Martin, *Brothers From Bataan* (Manhattan, Kans.: Sunflower University Press, 1992), p. 268.

Appendix 6: A Tribute by a Grandson

An essay by grandson Jeffrey John Blankman, originally written Nov. 12, 2001, for a speech-writing class at Northwestern University, assigned to compose a speech paying tribute to the character of a person he admired. (Prof. Huebner)

Edited and amended in April 2006 for presentation at my father's memorial service in Rochester, Minnesota, on April 24, 2006.

Ken Davis: Service, Strength, Simplicity

By Jeffrey Blankman

How does one pay adequate tribute to a great man? The few minutes and meager words that I have to fill them seem slight indeed. Slight in comparison to the greatness of my grandfather's character; slight in the face of the profound influence that he has had on so many people, including me.

To those of us who knew him, Kenneth Earl Davis was dedicated to service, a tall pillar of strength, and a practitioner of simplicity.

As a young man he saw the outbreak of World War II and enlisted voluntarily in the Army. He served his country for four years in the Pacific Theater, beginning in the Philippines. During this time he had the strength of mind and body to endure the Bataan Death March, the horrific death of his best army buddy, and three disease-filled, festering years in Japanese prison camps. Yet, he seemed to emerge from all of this unscathed. He harbored no grudge or bitterness in his heart after the war. In his unselfishly simple view he was just doing his duty: defending the world's freedom. Besides, it was through his war experience that what he later described as the best thing to ever happen to him came about—Grandma.

I love to recall that story the most, I think. It's so simple, so pure and old-school—it couldn't have been written better in a fairy tale—and it couldn't be more fitting to Grandpa. While recovering on a hospital bed another soldier on a neighboring bed showed him a picture of his sister. As the story goes, he fell in love at first sight and simply declared that he was going to marry her when he got home. Ever a man of his word, he did—and he loved her for a lifetime.

Back home, as a husband and father he served his family faithfully, in the best way he knew. He worked hard as a mechanic for the railroads, and later for a hospital, providing stability for his five children. His strength of character provided a model for all of them. I have never heard of a single instance when he lied or intentionally deceived anyone. He also taught them to have faith in God, as well as an understanding of those things in life which are truly important. He always imparted knowledge by example and through simple wisdom. Each day, just after saying grace, he would preface dinner by saying, "Take all you want, but eat all you take." He meant it, too.

As his grandson, I had ample opportunity to witness his service to others in his community. After retiring, he spent a good part of his time helping people in whatever way he could. He did things like fixing people's cars or furnaces. When there was a bat flying around the church it was Ken who got the call to come catch it, and when there were no distress calls to occupy him, he could be found in his garage workshop making wooden crafts for friends, or out on his pontoon teaching neighborhood kids how to fish.

I have many, many memories of my grandfather—many good, fond memories. Truly, I do not have a single bad one, and I can't even ever recall seeing him angry. Maybe that's why I remember him as some sort of superhero. Indeed, he had the physical strength and integrity of character that evokes images of Superman. In his sixties he was still one of the strongest men I knew. His chest and biceps were larger than those of most men one-third his age. Triple-bypass surgery did not seem to faze him in the least, physically or emotionally. He was under doctor's orders not to lift anything over ten pounds, but when the ice broke on the lake that spring he erected the dock by himself anyway.

I also remember his simple virtues and enduring optimism. He seemed to live for each day, taking nothing for granted. Perhaps he learned this from his war experiences. He found innumerable joys in something as simple as fishing. I loved to go with him, more than anything else in life, I think. He had such great patience. He'd spend the hours of waiting remarking on the beauty of the lake, or explaining the intricacies of angling. He knew by rote the location of every sandbar, by heart the depths of each part of the lake, and by name all the weeds I'd snag and reel in—just like he knew most everyone in his town, Nisswa. As we'd drive along on the way to someplace or another, he knew the names of all the people living in each house we passed, as well as the names of each family that had lived there since the house was built, *and* where they had worked when they lived there and why they had moved and where they had moved to. Because, at some point, he'd helped each and every one of them with something or other, and probably imparted some simple, optimistic wisdom along the way, too.

My grandfather may not have held office, invented anything like the light bulb, or conceived and implemented sweeping social change, *but he mattered to people, because people mattered to him.* His life was dedicated to service, founded firmly in physical and moral strength, and practiced with a simplicity that was transparent and easily understood by everyone with whom he came into contact. I am *so* proud to call you my grandfather. You truly were a great man.

Just a week or two ago one of my students asked me that age-old question. If I could spend a day with anybody in the world, living or dead, who would it be? At the time I don't think I had an answer, but now I know what I will say if anyone ever asks me again: I'd want to spend it with Grandpa, fishing.

Appendix 7: A Letter from a Friend

This letter was written by a friend to Ken Davis, Jr., son of Kenneth Earl Davis, after he learned about Ken Sr.'s WWII service and sacrifice. The letter was read at the memorial service of Kenneth Earl Davis.[73]

Dear Ken,   Thursday, August 18, 2005

They say that what you don't know won't hurt you. Truth is what you don't know can hurt you. Thank you. Because of you, I shook his hand. I sat as his dinner table. I rode in his car (an adventure all its own!). I only wish I'd known enough to tell him "Thanks."

You introduced me to him. It was really no big deal to me at the time. Another old man, hard to listen to, hard to understand. He seemed to be preoccupied the whole time I was around him. I watched you interact with him and it seemed difficult and awkward. He bounced from subject to subject and person to person. And yet, when I looked deeply I could see more. He loved you. And his appreciation for you, his daughters and his wife was deep. I watched him one day as you entertained a crowd in his hometown. He was proud, but not in a way that indicated surprise. He expected you to be at least as good as you were. He was sure of your success.

I wonder now about his secrets. I wonder how he suppressed his anxiety and fear. I wonder if the memories had faded, and pain worn off. It's no wonder that he could run a red light without fear. It's no wonder he could work quietly and patiently with his hands at his workbench.

Until recently, I didn't know what people meant when they called his generation, the Greatest Generation. How does one come to that conclusion? Now I understand... they were the greatest generation because they were men and women, who choose service over self, sacrifice over gratification, future over present, and principle over peace. It was the greatest generation and Mr. Davis epitomized it.

I never knew about...

　　　　him being abandoned by his country...

---

[73] Printed with permission of Danny DeArmis.

the sixty miles he walked …
the prison he lived in…
the meals he missed…
the beatings he endured…
the fear he felt…
the loneliness he suffered…
the despair he experienced…
the chains he wore…
the hope he'd lost…
the debt he paid so I can enjoy my pursuit of happiness.

If only I had known all of this, I would have thanked him myself. What I didn't know did hurt me… and cost me that opportunity.

Danny DeArmis

Appendix 8: Basic Information on Hazel Irene Brown

- Born in Kellihor, Minnesota at home, August 10, 1924
- Siblings: Lester Brown, Harriet Kramp, Alpheus Brown, Lucille Christiansen
    o Harriet and Al were both married at the same time as Hazel on February 20, 1946
- Moved to Iowa
- Father was a cement mason
- Lake Hubert 1st-6th grade (1930-37)
- 7th grade to Biwabik (1937-38)
    o Grandpa worked for WPA on bridge and dams as superintendent/blueprints man
- Lived at Lake Esquagama
- 8th grade in Orr (1938-39)
- Attended school in Cotton sometime in this period
- Lived on Nett Lake Indian Reservation 3 months February-April of 1940
- 9th grade Eveleth (1939-40)
- 10th grade Tower/Sedan (1940-41)
- 11th grade Pequot Lakes (1941-42)
- 12th grade St. Paul Mechanic Arts (1942-43)
- Father was a guard for shipbuilders
- Attended school in Duluth for a month
- Graduated Pequot Lakes 1943
    o Family lived in a small travel trailer with a double bunk–3 girls shared top and parents on the bottom
- All three brothers quit school and went to work

- Employment before marriage
    o Marten's (lunch place in Nisswa)
    o Vic's Master station attendant (bookkeeper)
    o S & H Auto Body (bookkeeping) until married

February 20, 1946	Married Kenneth Earl Davis
November 15, 1946	Kenneth Alpheus Davis born
July 26, 1948	Carol Ann Davis born

April 13, 1954	Kathy Irene Davis born
August 22, 1955	Candie Lynn Davis born
February 13, 1968	Kari Lee Davis born

- Employment after marriage
    o Secretary/bookkeeper Gino Paulucci Farms
    o Assistant to Clerk of Court, St. Peter, Minnesota

- Currently living at Shorewood Commons in Rochester, Minnesota

Information from conversation with Hazel in 1998 and again in 2010.

If you would like to book the WWII multi-media
presentation by Candie Blankman or have Candie speak at
your next event, contact her at candobando@gmail.com

Blog:
Candie.blankman@blogspot.com

Church website:
www.fpcdowney.com

Connect with Candie on Facebook and Twitter
FB: CandieBlankman
Twitter @candobando

Copies of Forged by War are available
on Amazon (www.amazon.com) or from author
Candie Blankman
PO Box 5069
Downey, CA 90241